MW00778452

Gleanings
in the
Fields of Boaz

WATCHMAN NEE
Translated from the Chinese

Christian Fellowship Publishers, Inc.
New York

ISBN 0-935008-68-3

Available from the Publishers at:

11515 Allecingie Parkway
Richmond, Virginia 23235

TRANSLATOR'S PREFACE

So rich were the fields of Boaz that even the gleanings from them were more than sufficient for the livelihood of Ruth and her mother-in-law, Naomi (see Ruth 2). God gave such abundance of revelation and utterance to Watchman Nee that in his several decades of active ministry numerous messages were delivered by him, mostly in speaking and some in writing. Many of these precious messages have been translated and published in English either in books or booklets. Yet there were still sheaves left in the field waiting to be gleaned. These were too valuable to be lost. Hence, the compilation of the contents of this book.

The contents of the first part of the book have been gathered from the English notes of a beloved sister in Christ who is now with the Lord. She took down copious notes as she listened to the author during the years 1939–1940. Some of the messages from this ministry were already previously published in various books, but a number of them from this period were left untouched. These have now been grouped together in the present volume and edited further under the three general subtitles "Live by the Life of God," "We Died in Christ," and "God's Building." The second part—entitled "Pulled-Out Sheaves"—is composed of two, thus far unpublished articles (the second of which has never appeared even in Chinese) together with the author's last exhortations to his fellow-workers at the conclusion of the Second Kuling Training Session (1949) and at a later time around 1950 or 1951. These are priceless. The third part is devoted to a collection of a few of the many letters written by the author which taken as a whole reveal him in a most intimate way as having been a faithful and choice servant of the Lord. They are invaluable.

Into God's hand is now committed this book. May His richest blessing be upon all its readers.

CONTENTS

PART ONE

FROM THE MINISTRY OF 1939-1940*

*Being a reproduction of the notes — taken down in English by a dear Christian sister now with the Lord — of several of the author's messages delivered in Chinese during this period, with no more than some necessary tidying up added. — *Translator*

1 | Live by the Life of God

A. LIVE BY THE WILL OF MAN OR BY THE LIFE OF GOD

Who hath been made, not after the law of a carnal commandment, but after the power of an endless life. (Heb. 7.16)

Fear not; I am the first and the last, and the Living one; and I was dead, and behold, I am alive for evermore, and I have the keys of death and of Hades. (Rev. 1.17b–18)

Whom God raised up, having loosed the pangs of death: because it was not possible that he should be holden of it. (Acts 2.24)

Watch and pray, that ye enter not into temptation: the spirit indeed is willing, but the flesh is weak. (Matt. 26.41)

Jesus said unto her, I am the resurrection, and the life: he that believeth on me, though he die, yet shall he live. (John 11.25)

That I may know him, and the power of his resurrection, and the fellowship of his sufferings, becoming conformed unto his death. (Phil. 3.10)

And what the exceeding greatness of his power to usward who believe, according to that working of the strength of his might which he wrought in Christ, when he raised him from the dead, and made him to sit at his right hand in the heavenly places. (Eph. 1.19–20)

It is God who worketh in you both to will and to work, for his good pleasure. (Phil. 2.13)

Whereunto I labor also, striving according to his working, which worketh in me mightily. (Col. 1.29)

We know that the law is spiritual: but I am carnal, sold under sin (Rom. 7.14)

We would not have you ignorant, brethren, concerning our affliction which befell us in Asia, that we were weighed down exceedingly, beyond our power, insomuch that we despaired even of life: yea, we ourselves have had the sentence of death within ourselves, that we should not trust in ourselves, but in God who raiseth the dead. (2 Cor. 1.8–9)

He hath said unto me, My grace is sufficient for thee: for my power is made perfect in weakness. (2 Cor. 12.9a)

Seeing that ye seek a proof of Christ that speaketh in me; who to you-ward is not weak, but is powerful in you. (2 Cor. 13.3)

Many people are living by their own will, not by the life of God. They are Christians because they have decided to be such. They have made a decision of the will. They want sanctification and are determined to have it. They have resolved to experience victory in their lives. Good as all these may appear, these people nonetheless are living by their wills. Their life is all within the circle of their own wills. Similarly, much Christian work is done also only in this realm.

You ought to be Christians, you ought to have victory, and you ought to be filled with the Spirit. But the absolute limit that you can reach is only to desire it. "The spirit indeed is willing, but the flesh is weak" (Matt. 26.41b). "For to will is present with me, but to do that which is good is not. For the good which I would I do not: but the evil which I would not, that I practise" (Rom. 7.18b-19). The desire of the will cannot give you the power to do it, for the flesh is stronger.

One who relies on the will is sure to be defeated. The will is too weak, it cannot get one there. It can only function insofar as something moves or pushes it. This is not the life of Christ; this is the life of the will. It is destined for defeat.

The life of Christ, however, is beyond the volition. His life carries us through; His life just naturally carries us along and takes us through. We do nothing; He does it all. His life flows and overflows the will and circumstances. We do not swim through, nor do we crawl through. We neither fight nor force our way. He simply carries us through in His arms.

In regard to our physical weaknesses, the same rule governs. We cannot force ourselves to overcome our weaknesses or live above them. But the life of Christ just flows on and carries us through. We need not pull ourselves together and push on, for Christ simply does it for us. As described in 2 Corinthians 1.8-9, Paul was in utter hopelessness both within and without. He was truly in a desperate condition with every hope gone. Then he declared that he trusted in the power that raised Jesus from among the dead. He trusted in the resurrection life of our Lord Jesus. Life is not enough, it must be resurrection life. Whereas Romans 7 shows us that the will is powerless — for it cannot take us through, Romans 8 tells us that "the law of the Spirit of life in Christ Jesus made me free from the law of sin and of death" (v.2).

B. LIVE BY THE WISDOM OF MAN OR BY THE LIFE OF GOD

Our glorying is this, the testimony of our conscience, that in holiness and sincerity of God, not in fleshly wisdom but in the grace of God, we behaved ourselves in the world, and more abundantly to you-ward. (2 Cor. 1.12)

And it came to pass, when he was come near to enter into Egypt, that he said unto Sarai his wife, Behold now, I know that thou art a fair woman to look upon: and it will come to pass, when the Egyptians shall see thee, that they will say, This is his wife: and they will kill me, but they will save thee alive. Say, I pray thee, thou art my sister; that it may be well with me for thy sake, and that my soul may live because of thee. (Gen. 12.11–13)

And it came to pass, on one of the days, as he was teaching the people in the temple, and preaching the gospel, there came upon him the chief priests and the scribes with the elders; and they spake, saying unto him, Tell us: By what authority doest thou these things? or who is he that gave thee this authority? And he answered and said unto them, I also will ask you a question; and tell me: The baptism of John, was it from heaven, or from men? And they reasoned with themselves, saying, If we shall say, From heaven; he will say, Why did ye not believe him? But if we shall say, From men; all the people will stone us: for they are persuaded that John was a prophet. And they answered, that they knew not whence it was. And Jesus said unto them, Neither tell I you by what authority I do these things. (Luke 20.1–8)

I am come down from heaven, not to do mine own will, but the will of him that sent me. (John 6.38)

We have seen that man's will is not the thing we live by. Now we shall see that neither is man's wisdom the governing principle of life either. Whoever acts on "policy" is on the wrong road. We should only ask, "What is the will of God?" Do not let our own cleverness become involved in it at all. Are you afraid of difficulty or trouble? If so, "policy" or human wisdom immediately makes its appearance. Do you seek the glory of men? If so, then "policy" slips in.

However, if you only want the will of God to be that which you follow (after His will is shown you), then you will not be moved by the criticism of man. Just specialize on the will of God. Never mind what the world or anyone else may think; nor consider what the consequences may be.

Do not trust in man's will or wisdom; trust only on the grace of God. When you have made a huge mistake—an "honorable mess"—simply cry to God, "Lord, have mercy and help me." Do not try to extricate yourself with more maneuverings, but cast yourself upon the mercy of God. He will disperse the clouds and deliver you.

It is the brilliant who get into the most trouble because they rely on their wisdom. The people who are far less bright have little trouble inasmuch as they have only God on whom to rely. But where there is "policy," there will always be crookedness, deceit and sin. Weighing the question, looking at the various sides to the question, figuring out what might happen if we say or do this or that—all this is pragmatic "policy." For the Christian, though, it is sin. God will not allow you to act and follow what *you* think, but to act and follow after His will. Sometimes you may feel as though you are heading straight toward something dreadful, but if this is *His* will and way, then do not reason but simply obey with childlike faith.

C. THE LAW OF THE SPIRIT OF LIFE

I delight in the law of God after the inward man: but

I see a different law in my members, warring against the law of my mind, and bringing me into captivity under the law of sin which is in my members. (Rom. 7.22–23)

The law of the Spirit of life in Christ Jesus made me free from the law of sin and of death. For what the law could not do, in that it was weak through the flesh, God, sending his own Son in the likeness of sinful flesh and for sin, condemned sin in the flesh: that the ordinance of the law might be fulfilled in us, who walk not after the flesh, but after the Spirit. (Rom. 8.2–4)

The man of Romans 7 is living by his will. His entire life and conduct are controlled by himself. Though his will may be good, his conduct is bad. He comforts himself by saying, "I want God; my will is on God's side; I hate sin, I do not want to do anything wrong; I want God's will and want to glorify Him in all things." Yet this is as far as that person's goodness goes. He has not seen that all this is in the realm of the will, that he has never gone beyond the will. For this reason, he is still under law. The power of his will becomes the sole power of his life; and thus he is not able to lift himself out of weakness into attainment.

Many Christians have themselves well in hand. They maintain a strong grip on themselves. They are determined not to sin nor to offend. They powerfully push and pull and control themselves in order to make themselves a certain kind of person who acts in a certain way and talks with a certain tone of voice which they approve or desire to be or have. They therefore force themselves to do what they do not want to do and suppress themselves under the power of the will. But all this is nothing but law, the law of the natural will. Yet Romans 8.2 tells us that "the law of the Spirit of life in Christ Jesus made me free from the law of sin and of death." If one is not experiencing it, it is either because he is not born again or he has not been well taught in the full gospel of Jesus Christ. What he knows is only an imperfect gospel, or else he does not really believe in God's word due to the lack of revelation.

How does the law of the Spirit of life overcome the law of sin and of death? The minute you are saved, you know what you ought to do. You do not have to weigh and reason as to whether a thing or action, word or attitude is right or wrong. There is something within you which tells you all. Therefore it is not a question of knowing, but rather a question of whether you obey that inner voice—that inner light—or not. The law of the Spirit of life is operating within you all the time, but you may not have learned to obey it. The way this law overcomes the other law is simply, naturally effortless. Because you recognize and believe this law of life which is operating within you, you simply lift up your eyes and say to the Lord, "Lord, I cannot; but You can." That is all. It is not by trying, but by recognizing that life in you which is Christ. You just watch it live and flow and operate naturally and without any effort at all.

Suppose you are once again invited to someone's house where heretofore you had always talked in the flesh and done things which did not glorify the Lord. Do you need to get yourself ready by praying much about it, resolving not to repeat what you said or did before, and crying to the Lord to help you? No, you merely believe that there is a new law working in you, even the law of the Spirit of life in Christ Jesus. And this law will set you free. Rest in the power of the law of life. Do not try, nor be anxious. Just leave everything to that life, to that law. And should you forget, the Spirit will remember; for that is His responsibility. The law is operating naturally and without effort. Trust Him with a childlike faith, free from effort, struggle, or working up the will.

Is there such a spontaneous law working in you? Is there a natural, easy, effortless, spontaneous life flowing out from you?

D. LET GO AND LET GOD

Behold the birds of the heaven, that they sow not, neither do they reap, nor gather into barns; and your heavenly Father feedeth them. Are not ye of much more value than they? And which of you by being anxious can add one cubit unto the measure of his life? And why are ye anxious concerning raiment? Consider the lilies of the field, how they grow; they toil not, neither do they spin: yet I say unto you, that even Solomon in all his glory was not arrayed like one of these. But if God doth so clothe the grass of the field, which today is, and to-morrow is cast into the oven, shall he not much more clothe you, O ye of little faith? (Matt. 6.26–30)

There is therefore now no condemnation to them that are in Christ Jesus. (Rom. 8.1)

There is a new law working in us that is greater than the old law. Believe in this new law. Believe that it is working, and it will work indeed. Simply follow that law. Such is the way Christians live.

Unsaved people, on the other hand, must hold on to themselves. They need to control and suppress and order their lives by their wills. The saved, though, can let go of themselves. They can take their hands off of themselves, can give up trying and struggling with their wills, and let go absolutely and utterly. They shall find themselves dropping into the hands of God. Let go and let God.

E. THE WORD OF GOD IS LIVING

The word of God is living, and active, and sharper than any two-edged sword, and piercing even to the dividing of soul and spirit, of both joints and marrow, and quick to discern the thoughts and intents of the heart. (Heb. 4.12)

Search me, O God, and know my heart: try me, and know my thoughts; and see if there be any wicked way in me, and lead me in the way everlasting. (Ps. 139.23–24)

The opening of thy words giveth light; it giveth understanding unto the simple. (Ps. 119.130)

All things when they are reproved are made manifest
by the light: for everything that is made manifest is light.
(Eph. 5.13)

Jacob called the name of the place Peniel: for, said
he, I have seen God face to face, and my life is preserved.
(Gen. 32.30)

In him was life; and the life was the light of men. (John
1.4)

How are we going to know what part of our
thoughts or our decisions is from God and what part
is our own? Sometimes there is only a hair-breadth difference; and hence we find we just cannot differentiate
them. We may ask ourselves, Is this myself, or the Lord,
in me? Is it from my spirit or from my soul? We try
to dissect our thoughts and words and acts in order to
know which part is natural and which part is spiritual.
This is a most difficult task, and we grow quite
desperate when trying to make the discrimination.

To try to do this is fatal. It only results in perplex-
ity and hesitation. Nothing is definite or settled; it is
like always being in a maze — or in a haze. But this whole
approach is wrong. God has never told us that we can
find within ourselves what is the soul and what is the
spirit. Such an approach is wrong and the person trying to do it is also wrong. God has never meant for
us to do this, because looking within will only result
in darkness. Self-examination in this regard will never
result in our finding the light. For all is dark inside us.
To follow this track will lead us nowhere. It is a blind
alley. So we must stop doing it.

"The word of God is living, and active, and sharper than any two-edged sword, and piercing even to the dividing of soul and spirit, of both joints and marrow, and quick to discern the thoughts and intents of the heart." When we say or feel we are right or wrong, the question becomes, How do we know it? From where came the light—that is to say, the knowledge of whether it is right or wrong? From within ourselves or from the word of God? Has there been revelation? There must be revelation or light on the basis of God's word so that we really see. The moment the Holy Spirit throws light on God's word, we see and we know.

We must have the light that kills. Under such light we see that everything about us is soulish. Hence revelation is what we need, because it slays and it does the work. Outside of revelation, God does no other work. It is enough when we obtain revelation, for then the work is done. The moment we receive revelation and see ourselves as God sees us, at that very moment we are weakened and our soul life dies. The light which comes from revelation brings with it power; or rather, it itself is power. So all depends on revelation. There is nothing left after that for God to do. There is no second step to take—revelation or light does it all. As they say at Honor Oak,* "Revelation will do the trick."

---

*The place name of the ministry and fellowship center in London where Mr. T. Austin-Sparks ministered.—*Author* Mr. Nee himself visited with the brethren there once in 1933 while on a trip to Britain and America that year; and on numerous occasions during a much longer stay in Britain and Europe in 1938–1939, he ministered the word of God among them.—*Translator*

As at Peniel, Jacob said, "I have seen God face to face." This is the place of revelation. It is not just an experience, it is a being face to face with God himself. It is not God's working; it is Light itself. Light kills, but better yet, light cleanses. The only reason we have not had the light is because we have had no room for it. We have shut the door. We are closed to it. Pray that we may be open to it. We shall not obtain the light until we are open to it. And when the light comes, it kills. Yet after we receive the light, we should never look within and ask ourselves if we are right or wrong, if this is soulish or spiritual. Only pray, "Search me, O God, and know my heart: try me, and know my thoughts; and see if there be any wicked way in me, and lead me in the way everlasting."

You should learn to open yourselves up. Do not deceive yourselves, nor be proud. Be humble and study to be sincere. Oftentimes we are not sincere with God and with His word. Sometimes the light comes slowly, only little by little. But when it comes, yield to it. Walk softly with fear and trembling. Deal with self to the uttermost limit, or rather, let the Holy Spirit deal with you without restraint. The reason we lack discernment with respect to other people's situations is because we have not allowed God to give us light about ourselves. We need to discern our own self first. Then we can help others to see.

2 | We Died in Christ

A. WE DIED IN CHRIST

Therefore, as through one man sin entered into the world, and death through sin; and so death passed unto all men, for all have sinned . . . But not as the trespass, so also is the free gift. For if by the trespass of the one the many died, much more did the grace of God, and the gift by the grace of the one man, Jesus Christ, abound unto the many. . . . So then as through one trespass the judgment came unto all men to condemnation; even so through one act of righteousness the free gift came unto all men to justification of life. For as through the one man's disobedience the many were made sinners, even so through the obedience of the one shall the many be made righteous. . . . that, as sin reigned in death, even so might

grace reign through righteousness unto eternal life through
Jesus Christ our Lord. (Rom. 5.12–21)

We know that the law is spiritual: but I am carnal,
sold under sin. For that which I do I know not: for not
what I would, that do I practise; but what I hate, that
I do. (Rom. 7.14–15)

God wants us not only to know our sins — as to what
they are — so that we may realize our sinful acts and
lives; He also wants us to know that we are sinners —
that quite apart from our sins we are innately, fundamentally, through and through sinners. We are by
nature sinners, we are constitutionally sinners. We are
born sinners before we commit any sinful act. Thank
God, the blood of our Lord Jesus which was shed on
Calvary's cross cleanses our *sins* away; but the blood
will never cleanse *us*. There was and is no forgiveness
for us as sinners. There is only the cross for us. When
Christ died on the cross, we died in Him and with Him.

Cleansing is most certainly to be found in the blood,
but this is for *sins*. For *us sinners* there is only *death*.
Our trouble today is not that we are not careful or that
we have weak wills. We are wrong because we do not
know ourselves. We fail to see that we are sold under
sin. It is not our *conduct*; it is *we ourselves* that constitutes the problem. God's way of salvation goes further than dealing with our sins, it deals also with us.
May God open our eyes to see that God has put us as
sinners into Christ and has caused us to die in His death.
"It is finished" (John 19.30b).

B. IN CHRIST OR IN ADAM

Now consider how great this man [Melchizedek] was, unto whom Abraham, the patriarch, gave a tenth out of the chief spoils. And they indeed of the sons of Levi that receive the priest's office have commandment to take tithes of the people according to the law, that is, of their brethren, though these have come out of the loins of Abraham: but he whose genealogy is not counted from them hath taken tithes of Abraham, and hath blessed him that hath the promises. But without any dispute the less is blessed of the better. And here men that die receive tithes; but there one, of whom it is witnessed that he liveth. And, so to say, through Abraham even Levi, who receiveth tithes, hath paid tithes; for he was yet in the loins of his father, when Melchizedek met him. (Heb. 7.4–10)

Of him [God] are ye in Christ Jesus, who was made unto us wisdom from God, both righteousness and sanctification and redemption. (1 Cor. 1.30 mg.)

What shall we say then? Shall we continue in sin, that grace may abound? God forbid. We who died to sin, how shall we any longer live therein? Or are ye ignorant that all we who were baptized into Christ Jesus were baptized into his death? (Rom. 6.1–3)

Romans 5 shows us we are in Adam; Romans 6 tells us we are in Christ. Romans 7 exposes the fact of how we yet live in the flesh, whereas Romans 8 educates us about how to live in the Spirit.

Whenever we live in the flesh, everything we get from Adam is there. But if we live in the Spirit, then all that is in Christ becomes ours. Hence we need revelation as to how we are in Christ and to believe it. Then we must yield to the Holy Spirit and obey Him in order to live according to the Spirit and experience all that is in Christ.

Many Christians, however, fail to realize that they are in Adam. Therefore they see no need of being delivered out of him. They think that after their sins are forgiven, all their problems now lie in their behavior. They do not see that the real issue is in themselves.

How many of us reason that if we can only change our habits, ways, thoughts, acts, and so forth, we will be all right. Not so, however; for there must be a complete exchange of life. *We* must be displaced and replaced with *Christ*. We must see that whether we win or not, we ourselves are rotten and vile, altogether Adamic. Fundamentally speaking, we share Adam's very life. We are born of Adam. We are by nature Adamic.

How does God treat us little Adams? "He that hath died is justified [or, released, mg.] from sin" (Rom. 6.7). How did we get into Adam in the first place? Whose responsibility is it that we are in Adam? Whose fault and by whose work do we obtain this sinful nature of Adam? We can trace all this back to one person, Adam himself. All was done by Adam, not by us individually. In the same way, we get free of Adam and receive a new life with a new nature through another Person and His work.

When Adam ate the forbidden fruit in the Garden

of Eden, we were there in the loins of Adam. We too ate of it and failed God. We disobeyed God and sinned against Him. The entity and the solidarity of the human race come to the fore here. Just so is it also with our righteousness received from Christ and our being in Christ: "of him [God] are ye in Christ Jesus." Because God has put us in Christ, all which God has done in Christ, all which He has given to Christ—even all the work and nature of Christ—become ours.

If we look within ourselves, we cannot see how we were in Adam; therefore we cannot believe it. Likewise, if we look within ourselves, we cannot see how we are in Christ. Accordingly, we must look away from ourselves and look off to Christ. We must see ourselves in Christ there at Calvary. For by looking within ourselves, we will never believe that we have been crucified and have died. All we see will be our sins, defeats and failure. But if we look at Christ and see ourselves in Him, we will know that we have died in spite of what we may see within ourselves or what our life experiences tell us. Hence it all depends on whether or not we have seen this glorious fact, whether or not our eyes have been opened to see ourselves being in Christ. It is not that we are "identified" with Christ, but that we actually are "included" in Christ. This requires revelation. With revelation everything will change.

The word does not say, "Abide *into* Christ." It says, "Abide *in* Christ." We are already there in Christ. Do not get out. Satan tries to get us to look at our life, experiences and defeats in order to say to us that we are not in Christ. We should never say a word or entertain a thought which even approaches our not being in Christ. We must hold unwaveringly, absolutely and tenaciously to the glorious reality that we are in Christ at all times.

C. HE THAT IS DEAD IS FREE FROM SIN

He that hath died is justified [or, free] from sin. (Rom. 6.7)

Some sins are on the outside, outward; some sins are on the inside, inward. There are sins of one's outward life, and there are sins of the conscience. We can never know what sin really is until God's light shines in. Then our conscience is awakened and begins to feel the awfulness of it. We now realize we are vile and full of sins; nevertheless, we are helpless because sin has power over us. We begin to feel miserable and desire to be forgiven and delivered. This is the first step toward salvation. Through the enlightenment of the Holy Spirit we see that Jesus Christ has died for our sins; therefore heaven's gate is now open to us. This is Romans chapters 1 to 5.

But many people have experienced only a half salvation, because they only know that God has forgiven their sins and cleansed their conscience, but do not know that He has also broken the power of sin in their lives. They fail to understand that the root problem of their lives lies not in what they do but in what they are in themselves. This can be likened to a fountain pen that leaks. It is futile to clean up the spilled ink instead of stopping the leak. We imagine that the fault is in our evil surroundings, in the strength of our temptations, in our not being careful or watchful, or in our being too easy with ourselves; whereas the real issue is not in any of these things but is in ourselves. For we ourselves are wrong, our very being is wrong. Our "self" is sinful. For example, if one's pocket has a hole in it, things in the pocket will naturally fall out. It is not a matter of whether or not one is careful, but that the pocket has a hole in it. In like manner, we sin not because we are being tempted and careless; we sin because that is just the way we are. *We* are sinful, and so we sin.

Romans 1.1 to 5.11 deals with outward sins as well as sins of the conscience. How does God deal with these sins? He uses the blood of Jesus to cleanse our conscience as well as to atone for our sins. Nevertheless, the blood never cleans our old man or natural life. Our old man is condemned to death. It cannot be cleansed, for it is too rotten, vile and hopeless. If a thing can still be patched or mended, built up or strengthened, we will do it. Not until it gets to the state of being totally hopeless will we throw it away and get a new one. Our old man with its heart and natural life is beyond repair, patching up or mending. And hence, God simply discards it and replaces it with a new man with a new heart and His own life.

Since we cannot be repaired or fixed up, why not give up trying? We must come to the place where we see it is absolutely useless to try any further, for we have tried every means possible, but the old life still breaks out. It still manifests itself in sinning. We then acknowledge that we are sinful—innately so, inherently so, through and through. Until we see this there is no deliverance for us. We are not just sinful, full of sins, but we have a sinful nature. There is a law in us that must sin; it can do nothing else. Hence it is not simply that we *do* wrong, but that we *are* wrong. What is sin? It is the old nature in us.

Hence death is the only way out: "He that has died is free from sin." Death is the only exit from self. It is the only way of deliverance from the power of sin. One who has died sins no more: the liar lies no more; the thief steals no more; the irritable and angry man gets angry no more. Let us see, though, that the death of the physical body cannot free us from sin. The rich man in Hades still despised and looked down on Lazarus. He had not changed at all. His sins went right on in the next world (see Luke 16.19–31). Only the death of the "old man" brings about a complete change. This death is a wonderful, mysterious, glorious, miraculous death, for it changes all things. It accomplishes what physical death cannot do. Without this death there is no release from sin. Without it, there is no victory. But with it there is full and complete salvation, since it does away with the old man; that is to say, it does away with *me*.

How does this death come about? Thank God, it has all been done on the cross of Christ. God has wrapped me up in the death of Christ. He saw to it that I was done away with there, and that my execution was enacted. And this is what baptism stands for. When one is baptized it simply means that he was included in Christ's death. There he was wiped out on the cross. This is his testimony. "Lord, let me see this!"

D. LIFE OR DEATH

Out of the ground made Jehovah God to grow every tree that is pleasant to the sight, and good for food; the tree of life also in the midst of the garden, and the tree of the knowledge of good and evil. . . . But of the tree of the knowledge of good and evil, thou shalt not eat of it: for in the day that thou eatest thereof thou shalt surely die. (Gen. 2.9,17)

Since then the children are sharers in flesh and blood, he also himself in like manner partook of the same: that through death he might bring to nought him that had the power of death, that is, the devil. (Heb. 2.14)

If ye live after the flesh, ye must die; but if by the Spirit ye put to death the deeds of the body, ye shall live. (Rom. 8.13)

But hath now been manifested by the appearing of our Saviour Christ Jesus, who abolished death, and brought life and immortality to light through the gospel. (2 Tim. 1.10)

Since by man came death, by man came also the resurrection of the dead. For as in Adam all die, so also in Christ shall all be made alive. . . . For he must reign, till he hath put all his enemies under his feet. The last enemy that shall be abolished is death. . . . O death, where is thy victory? O death, where is thy sting? (1 Cor. 15.21–22,25–26,55)

Then shall the King say unto them on his right hand, Come, ye blessed of my Father, inherit the kingdom prepared for you from the foundation of the world. (Matt. 25.34)

Narrow is the gate, and straitened the way, that leadeth unto life, and few are they that find it. (Matt. 7.14)

The battle in this world is the battle for life. When God created man, a new species of being came into existence. Man as created was created to rule all the rest of creation for God. But he lost his dominion.

God put two trees in the Garden of Eden. One was the tree of life; the other was the tree of the knowledge of good and evil. This last we can call the tree of death as opposed to the tree of life, since on the day that one would eat of it he would die. Here we see the difference between God and Satan. God has the power of life, whereas Satan has the power of death. God scatters life, but Satan scatters death. Sometimes we tend to overestimate sin, in that we forget that Satan uses sin to bring in death. It is death he is after. Many people say there is something wrong with the world. Yes, but it is more than sin, it is death. Satan's whole aim and purpose is to effect death.

We see the two trees in the Garden. They show us that the controversy between God and Satan is one of life and death. The question between God and man is also one of life and death. And in Eden Satan has apparently accomplished his purpose.

If our gospel preaching and work only deal with the question of sin and fail to deal with death, they are a failure. For God's salvation deals with death as well as with sin. With the first Adam, it was sin, and then it was death. With all the rest of us in Adam, it is the same thing: death, then sin. The fountainhead or root is death; sin comes as its natural result. The moment man fell, Satan recovered the power he had lost, which is death. "Through death he [Christ] might bring to nought him [Satan] that had the power of death, that is, the devil; and might deliver all them [men] who through fear of death were all their lifetime subject to bondage" (Heb. 2.14–15). Satan uses death to govern man. Wherever you find Satan's power, there you find death. There is a principle here: whenever you see Satan working you will find death. Not particularly nor especially sin, for sin is not most centrally typical of Satan; but death is.

In so-called God's work, you may find peace and harmony with people seemingly able to work together, yet death is lurking there. Satan has a foothold there. This is always his particular work, especially now. Everything may seem peaceful, things are getting on nicely, no problem or trouble is in view, yet death is lurking in the background. Or in another work, where the flesh is active and problems are many, there may nonetheless be life there. It is all a question of life and death. Life is not a doctrine. It is not good thinking nor good feeling. It is not a matter of the mind or the emotion. It is not warmth. Life cannot be explained; it has to be experienced.

Satan governs the earth by means of death, but our Lord Jesus overcame Satan by means of that very thing — death. The death which Satan gives appears to be lasting and irreversible, but the death of Christ finishes everything that is outside of the realm of God. It conquers death itself, it makes death itself cease. You can burn cloth, paper, wood, and so forth, but you cannot burn ashes. Christ's death was a tremendous one, because in His death all deaths were included. As the sacrifice, He was utterly consumed; nothing was left except ashes. You cannot burn ashes again. His death was final. So death is forever and ever done away with. Because we have been united with Christ in His death, we have died in His death. Death can no longer touch us. What has been burnt up has been burnt up. There is no more death possible. So that the life we have in Christ Jesus is a life over which death has no power.

The question in Eden is the same question at Golgotha — a matter of life and death. The power of death came into Satan's hands in Eden, but Christ Jesus recovered this power over death on the cross. The controversy between God and Satan over life and death did not end in Eden, nor did it end at Golgotha. It continues on to the present day. It will only be settled when Satan is bound and cast into the abyss. His work today is still that of bringing in death whenever and wherever he can.

"The minding of the flesh is death" (Rom. 8.6,

Greek original). Whenever the flesh is given a place, there is death. The quickest and easiest way of spreading death is through conversation. One can become sick to death of all the talk one hears. Talking too much, criticizing, saying things out of ourselves — that is to say, the natural man expressing himself, exaggerating a bit, saying to people nice things which are untrue, speaking of things when one has no right to speak, or telling what one knows when it would be best to keep silent — all these are simply the flesh expressing itself. And all this simply scatters death. When we do any of these, we are Satan's co-workers. He is using us to bring in death.

Other Christians know and feel at once when we come near whether we bring life or death. Our spirits meet people even before our bodies get there. We can deceive ourselves, but we can never deceive others. They sense it at once.

First, where there is sin there is death. Second, whenever oneself is being expressed there is death. Anything out of self or the natural always spreads death. Third, wherever there is any expression of in-dividualistic life apart from the body of Christ, there is a scattering of death. A person can either spread death or life in a believers meeting. Hence each member of the body of Christ has a responsibility to the rest of the body.

The controversy today is the same as was in Eden, the same as was at Golgotha — life or death. What we want to see among us in this testimony is not teaching but life. Let us see that this question has been settled — and more than settled — on the cross. "The last enemy that shall be abolished is death." Death is also the first enemy to be conquered. The kingdom stands for life: "For narrow is the gate, and straitened the way, that leadeth unto life." In the time of the kingdom, not only sin shall be under the feet of Christ, death too shall be vanquished. The kingdom is to be a time of life, a time when death is bound. Yet we are to taste the kingdom life of Christ even now (cf. Heb. 6.5).

E. BAPTISM AS AN ANSWER TO GOD

> And now why tarriest thou? arise, and be baptized, and wash away thy sins, calling on his name. (Acts 22.16)
>
> I would not, brethren, have you ignorant, that our fathers were all under the cloud, and all passed through the sea; and were all baptized unto Moses in the cloud and in the sea. (1 Cor. 10.1–2)
>
> Are ye ignorant that all we who were baptized into Christ Jesus were baptized into his death? (Rom. 6.3)

In these three passages we will see the meaning of baptism. Baptism is "not the putting away of the filth of the flesh, but the interrogation of a good conscience toward God, through the resurrection of Jesus Christ" (1 Peter 3.21). Since it is an inquiry or demand of a good conscience towards God, it is therefore an answer to

God. God must therefore be asking a question. The answer to His question is an act, which is baptism. It is logical for us to believe that the question God asks is also formulated in an act—in the cross. What God asks of the believer is the following three-fold inquiry: (1) Look at the cross where My Son was crucified for your sins; what is your response to it? (2) I have included you in the death of Christ; you were nailed with Him there on the cross; what is your answer to this? and (3) Having been given such a wonderful Savior, what is to be your attitude to Him hereafter?

Baptism is our answer to all three parts of this question. It is our answer to the cross. First of all, God placed the sins of us, the worst persons in the world, upon Jesus, the best person in the world. The blood of Jesus washes all our sins away. What have we got to say to this? Our answer is "Baptize me." Baptism is the answer of a good conscience towards the matter of sins. If one is baptized, he must know that the blood of Jesus has washed all his sins away. God puts a representative thing before us—the cross; and we, too, put a representative thing before Him as our answer—baptism. Baptism is our response to God, embodied in an act. Though we say nothing, God understands, the angels understand, and even Satan understands. This act of confession reaches God, who also accepts it.

Secondly, God declares that it is not only our sins but even ourselves whom He has nailed to the cross with Christ. We are altogether rotten and sinful, and therefore He can do nothing with us except to finish us on the cross. How do we respond to that? Again, our answer is baptism. Since I have died with Christ,

I will be baptized to show that I am baptized into His death. I am rotten and vile, from inside to outside; there is no hope for me; and hence, I must be eliminated. Thank God, in Christ I died, I am finished.

And thirdly, having the issues of my sins and my self settled through the blood and the death of Christ (for His blood has cleansed me from my sins and His death has eliminated me), what should be my attitude towards Christ from now on? Once more, I answer with baptism. For in baptism I am baptized into Christ. From now on "it is no longer I that live, but Christ liveth in me" (Gal. 2.20). Whatever Christ does I do. His all becomes my all. His power becomes my power; His glory, my glory. All that He is and all that He does become mine, even my very life. We have become one. No one sees me anymore; all only see Him.

Baptized into Christ. What shall I do with such a Savior? What will be my life from now on? My answer is certain: from this moment on Christ becomes my aim, my goal, my Lord, my life, my all. I live for Him alone, not for the world nor for self, but wholly and only for Him. Baptism is like the "second edition" of Calvary, that is, it is my personal version of Calvary.

F. BAPTIZED UNTO HIS DEATH

We who died to sin, how shall we any longer live therein? Or are ye ignorant that all we who were baptized

into Christ Jesus were baptized into his death? (Rom.
6.2–3)

I delivered unto you first of all that which also I
received: that Christ died for our sins according to the
scriptures; and that he was buried; and that he hath been
raised on the third day according to the scriptures. (1 Cor.
15.3–4)

We were buried therefore with him through baptism
into death. (Rom. 6.4a)

Baptism is burial. What is the condition for burial?
It is death. We are not baptized in order to produce
death; no, we die first, and therefore we are baptized.
We have been grafted into Christ. This can be likened
to the transaction wherein the white skin of a foreign
nurse is grafted onto the arm of a Chinese woman and
thus becomes part of the latter. It has the same sensa-
tion, though it is of a different color. We have been
grafted into Christ so completely that we can never be
separated from Him. Whatever happens to Him happens to us. Whatever concerns Him concerns us. Every
feeling, every reaction and every move of His is also
ours because we are grafted into Him.

The ingrafting took place at the cross, where God
had put us into Christ: "But of him [God] are ye in
Christ Jesus, who was made unto us wisdom from God,
both righteousness and sanctification and redemption"
(1 Cor. 1.30 mg.). Poor, weak, futile, limited, poverty-
stricken, useless, ugly, and little, we nonetheless have
been grafted into the great, rich, powerful, mighty, fruitful, glorious, holy, victorious and perfect Christ. I have

lost my life utterly, wholly and completely in His. I no longer live apart from Him. I have no existence except in Him. I have died with Him. It is no longer I who live, but Christ who lives in me.

G. THE CROSS—THE SECRET OF LIFE

I also say unto thee, that thou art Peter, and upon this rock I will build my church; and the gates of Hades shall not prevail against it. (Matt. 16.18)

My heart was glad, and my tongue rejoiced; moreover my flesh also shall dwell in hope: because thou wilt not leave my soul unto Hades, neither wilt thou give thy Holy One to see corruption. (Acts 2.26–27)

O death, where is thy victory? O death, where is thy sting? (1 Cor. 15.55)

[I am] the Living one; and I was dead, and behold, I am alive for evermore, and I have the keys of death and of Hades. (Rev. 1.18)

Death and Hades were cast into the lake of fire. This is the second death, even the lake of fire. (Rev. 20.14)

Sheol cannot praise thee, death cannot celebrate thee: they that go down into the pit cannot hope for thy truth. The living, the living, he shall praise thee, as I do this day. (Is. 38.18–19a)

In him dwelleth all the fulness of the Godhead bodily. (Col. 2.9)

Whoso toucheth anything that is unclean by the dead. (Lev. 22.4b)

If Christ is in you, the body is dead because of sin; but the spirit is life because of righteousness. (Rom. 8.10)

Unto us God revealed them through the Spirit: for the Spirit searcheth all things, yea, the deep things of God. For who among men knoweth the things of a man, save the spirit of the man, which is in him? even so the things of God none knoweth, save the Spirit of God. But we received, not the spirit of the world, but the spirit which is from God; that we might know the things that were freely given to us of God. Which things also we speak, not in words which man's wisdom teacheth, but which the Spirit teacheth; combining spiritual things with spiritual words. Now the natural man receiveth not the things of the Spirit of God: for they are foolishness unto him; and he cannot know them, because they are spiritually judged. (1 Cor. 2.10–14)

When we touch Christ we touch God. The church is more than a company of forgiven sinners. She is the body of Christ, the fullness of Him who fills all in all. Why has the church been formed and left in the world? — to be a people for the Lord's own possession and to worship the Son. What is distinctively unique about the fullness of Christ? The specialty of Christ is demonstrated in what He says of himself, namely, "I am the life," "I am the resurrection and the life." He is far more than being Savior, Shepherd, Lord, Leader, King, and so forth. He is all these and more. He declares, "I am the first and the last, and the Living one; and I was dead, and behold, I am alive for ever-more, and I have the keys of death and of Hades." This is the special, central thing about Christ. The reason why the church can express Christ's life and resurrec-tion is because she knows that life, that resurrection life.

The central, pivotal, special or peculiar nature of everything that comes from God is life. And the cen-tral, special or peculiar nature of everything that comes from Satan is death. Whenever we touch and feel life, sense and see life in any form of expression, we know God is there. This life can go through any death and will always come out in resurrection. The main object in Christ's coming was not to secure forgiveness or give holiness, but to bring life and life abundant. John 3 tells us of the new-born life; John 4, the water of life; John 5 and 6, the bread of life; John 7, the rivers of life; John 8, the light of life; and John 11, the resurrec-tion life.

The church as the body of Christ is merely a vessel for holding fast the Head as well as for containing the life of Christ. Even as Christ was the vessel for con-taining and manifesting the life of God, so the church is the vessel for containing and giving out the life of Christ. Thus we can easily understand where the at-tack of Satan will be aimed at and why. Some people think the ground we give for Satan's entrance is in the area of worldliness; yet even if the world is cut off, Satan may still enter in. Some think sin is the entrance point for Satan; yet even if there be no sin left, Satan can still gain entrance and obtain the victory. Accordingly, there is but one entrance, which is "the gates of Hades"—death. Of the church Christ says that "the gates of Hades shall not prevail against it." After King Hezekiah recovered from his sickness he in essence proclaimed a song of praise when he declared: "I said, In the noontide of my days I shall go into the gates of Sheol: I am deprived of the residue of my years. I said, I shall not see Jehovah, even Jehovah, in the land of the living: . . . What shall I say? he hath both spoken unto me, and himself hath done it: . . . but thou hast in love to my soul delivered it from the pit of corruption; for thou hast cast all my sins behind thy back" (Is. 38.10–17).

The whole question revolves around what is life and what is death. The reason we cannot distinguish between these two is because our natural life has not been dealt with. We cannot tell whether there is warmth or coldness. We cannot judge whether there is fruit or not. We cannot distinguish between life and death. We cannot discern what is spiritual life and what is soulish life, which latter thing is actually death.

It is not enough to know that Satan uses death as his method and weapon of attack; we must also know what death is. Romans 8.10 says: "if Christ is in you, the body is dead because of sin; but the spirit is life because of righteousness." From this we see that whatever comes forth from the Spirit (that is, from the Spirit in our spirit) is life, but whatever comes forth from the body is death. John 12.25 declares: "He that loveth his life [his soul] loseth it; and he that hateth his life [his soul] in this world shall keep it unto life eternal." Whatever comes forth from the soul-life is death. The body, under the control of the soul, delights to run here and there in ceaseless activity. The tongue without ceasing talks of things it ought not to talk about. It is all death. Only that which comes forth from the Spirit is life. The tongue may indeed speak of spiritual things, but it is speaking of things the mind knows with a natural gift of articulation. It is still death nonetheless. Many people have fine minds. They can think and weigh pros and cons. But this is still out from the soulish or natural life; and hence, it is still death.

One may be very active, but unless this activity is utterly and wholly out from the cross, it is death. Wherever the cross is, there is life. Wherever natural life is undealt with, there is death. We must distinguish between feelings and life, between being helped in the realm of the soul and life.

Wherever we see any element or aspect or working of death we must say, "I cut if off, Lord, I will not have it." We must learn to recognize the flesh when we see it and to recognize the cross working. Unless the cross has dealt deeply in us and is cutting, we cannot recognize the flesh in another. But when the day comes that the Lord touches our life bone and puts it out of joint, when the day comes that the backbone of our natural life has been broken, when we are weakened and have no more strength left, and when we go limping in fear and trembling, then — and only then — shall we know instinctively what is life and what is death.

3 | God's Building

A. GOD'S BUILDING

According to the grace of God which was given unto
me, as a wise master builder I laid a foundation; and
another buildeth thereon. But let each man take heed how
he buildeth thereon. For other foundation can no man
lay than that which is laid, which is Jesus Christ. But if
any man buildeth on the foundation gold, silver, costly
stones, wood, hay, stubble; each man's work shall be made
manifest: for the day shall declare it, because it is revealed
in fire; and the fire itself shall prove each man's work of
what sort it is. If any man's work shall abide which he
built thereon, he shall receive a reward. If any man's work
shall be burned, he shall suffer loss: but he himself shall
be saved; yet so as through fire. (1 Cor. 3.10-15)

The foundation is always the same. God himself has laid it: and it is Jesus Christ himself. But the building differs according to the difference in materials and workmanship. There is no building except Christ be the foundation; yet many of God's servants use wood, hay and stubble, while some use gold, silver and precious stones. God does not and will not ask how large a building you have built, or how clever or speedy or ornate you built it; instead, He asks what materials you have used.

It is not enough just to give mental assent to this truth. Even this understanding of yours may be wood, hay and stubble. The point is, are you using gold, silver and precious stones? Gold speaks of the nature of God, all that God does, all that is from God, and the glory of God. If God is doing it all, naturally all the glory goes back to God. Man gets glory only when he is mixed up in it. Silver speaks of redemption. We know all our works are based on and hinge upon the cross. Precious stones represent the work of the Holy Spirit. So here we see the complete cycle of what our materials should be.

On the other hand, wood speaks of man and his nature. It stands in contrast to gold, which represents God and His nature. Hay speaks of the works of man. "All flesh is grass, and all the goodliness thereof is as the flower of the field. The grass withereth, the flower fadeth, because the breath of Jehovah bloweth upon it; surely the people is grass" (Is. 40.6–7). Hay will be burnt up; hence all that is of the flesh will be destroyed. Stubble represents the weakness of man, the deadness and uselessness of the natural life.

The one who uses gold, silver and precious stones knows God as Father; he knows the cross subjectively as well as objectively so that all that he is and has has been through death; and he also knows that if anything is done it must be the work of the Holy Spirit.

Many times someone wants you to help him, or rather you want to help someone spiritually. And the question immediately arises, "What is my motive? Do I get a bit of comfort or ease or pleasure myself? Am I doing this just to be doing something? Am I going to get something later?" If so, you will not be able to help anyone because the cross has not been applied to your secret desire. Your desire has not gone through death. Sometimes you may feel led to go and talk to someone. You know what you are to say, yet you go beyond that and say more. True, the cross has been applied and has cut off what is not of God; nevertheless, it has not done its complete work. With the result that you say what God gives you plus some more words of your own.

The precious stones signify what has been first inwrought in us and then manifested in life and words to others. Stubble, though, is very plentiful. Many Christian workers are laboring mainly by their feelings. When they feel good, hot, and close to God, they work hard for Him. But if they feel cold, tired, dull, or indifferent, they do nothing. Hot or cold is still all a matter of themselves. All is useless because all is based on feeling. The material used is stubble.

Many others use only the material of the flesh; that is, brain power, cleverness, articulation, expressiveness, resourcefulness and ability. But all these are hay. The flesh is earthly, not heavenly. All which comes from the flesh will be burned up. All is natural. God will bring into the light the strongest, the most central and the most distinctive feature of each one's flesh and weaken it.

Wood represents that which is human. It is earthy, of the earth. Most of the so-called Christian works we see have the feel of earthiness about them. They never came forth from God. As to preaching the gospel, people assume that as long as the gospel is preached it does not make much difference who preaches it or how one preaches it. For is it not the gospel that counts? And does not the word of the gospel perform the work? But no, God wants to see who preaches the gospel, through whose hands it goes forth, in whose strength it is preached, who sends him out to preach, and what materials he uses in giving out the gospel. There must not be any mixture of earth in the preaching of the gospel. It must all be of gold.

Gold, silver and precious stones are costly. Wood, hay and stubble cost us little. Would to God that some people would only talk a little less about spiritual things, inasmuch as their lives and their words just do not tally. They are not what they talk about.

Then there is also a difference in weight. Wood, hay and stubble are very light by comparison, whereas gold, silver and precious stones are substantial and weighty. How much do we really "weigh" spiritually? How much does our work weigh before God? Most of us and much of our work are most likely very light and insubstantial.

B. THE CHURCH GIVEN THE KEYS OF THE KINGDOM OF HEAVEN

> I also say unto thee, that thou art Peter, and upon this rock I will build my church; and the gates of Hades shall not prevail against it. I will give unto thee the keys of the kingdom of heaven: and whatsoever thou shalt bind on earth shall be bound in heaven; and whatsoever thou shalt loose on earth shall be loosed in heaven. (Matt. 16.18–19)

Peter's confession (recorded in the preceding verses to these above) is based on the revelation which he received. What God has revealed is His Son himself as well as His work. This Jesus of Nazareth is really the Son of God, the Messiah, the Anointed One. Upon this revelation the Lord declares He will build His church. As a matter of fact, He declares two things with two "I will's": (1) "Upon this rock [upon this revelation] I will build my church"; and (2) "I will give unto thee the keys of the kingdom of heaven."

The foundation of the church is the confession based on the revelation that Jesus is the Christ, the Son of the living God. Peter first confessed: "Thou art the Christ" (v.16). Then the Lord said, "Thou art Peter, and upon this rock I will build my church." It is not enough to have only one Peter (a stone or a little rock); there must be many, many Peters (many little rocks), else the church cannot be built. These will be multitudes who have the same revelation and who make the same confession that Jesus is the Christ, the Son of the living God. Such revelation changes a Simon into a Peter. Without this revelation, a person can never be one of the many small rocks which make up the church. This revelation produces new birth. This is eternal life, for eternal life is knowing Jesus as the Christ, the Son of God. The church of Christ as a whole possesses this revelation; but each individual believer has his own personal revelation of the Rock—Christ himself, thus transforming him into a small rock and making him part of the church. The church is a company of people who know Christ to be what God knows Him to be.

Due to the twin facts that He is the Rock and you are a small rock, the Lord can then declare: "I will give unto thee the keys of the kingdom of heaven." This means the church is to keep the door shut against all that issues from Hades so that not one bit of it can get into the church and the kingdom. "The kingdom of heaven" is a dispensation during which the kingdoms of this world shall become the kingdom of our Lord and of His Christ (see Rev. 11.15). It is a time when Christ will reign in power and authority, and righteousness shall rule over the earth. It is a time when all powers will be His, and everything will be under His control.

But when Jesus first came to earth, He said, as John the Baptist had said, that "the kingdom of heaven is at hand" (Matt. 4.17). Yet He also said that "the kingdom of God is within you [or, in the midst of you, mg.]" (Luke 17.21). So that Bible scholars who have no revelation, but only brain-power, become confused. The answer is, however, that the Millennium is the kingdom, historically speaking (Matt. 4.17); but Jesus (in Luke

17.21) is speaking geographically: wherever the Lord Jesus is, there is the kingdom: wherever He is, there is kingdom ground: kingdom atmosphere comes and kingdom power prevails wherever He is present. Historically speaking, the kingdom of heaven lies in the future; it is yet to come. But Jesus has already given the keys of the kingdom of heaven to us. He wants us to open the doors of the kingdom to release all that is of the kingdom into the very place that we now occupy.

"Whatsoever thou shalt bind on earth shall be bound in heaven; and whatsoever thou shalt loose on earth shall be loosed in heaven." We are to bind here on earth whatever comes from Hades so that kingdom life can replace it. We are to loose here on earth whatever is of the kingdom so that kingdom glory may be manifested. God puts the church here to rule, to exercise authority and to reign, but the church has failed to do so. The church is supposed to open the gates of heaven, to loose kingdom conditions and blessings, and to bind the powers of Hades. In this respect earth controls heaven. Earth binds first, then heaven binds. Earth looses first, and then heaven looses. Thus, incredibly as it may seem, heaven is limited by earth.

Such, then, is our work here on earth. We have been given authority and power to bind all that is not of heaven and to loose all that is of heaven. Whenever we see that the gates of Hades have pushed in and taken possession of what belongs to God, we are here to oppose that. We are to take the keys of the kingdom and loose heaven's power against it. The reason why there is so little of the kingdom here is because the church has not used the keys the Lord has given to her. The keys are given to all who can be trusted to use them faithfully and rightly. "Whatsoever"—this signifies that all which is of the kingdom and all which is of heaven are at our disposal if we only loose them. He has given the keys of the kingdom of heaven to us, and is waiting for us to use them.

C. THE CHURCH AS REPRESENTATIVE OF GOD'S AUTHORITY

Thus saith Jehovah to his anointed, to Cyrus, whose right hand I have holden, to subdue nations before him, and I will loose the loins of kings; to open the doors before him, and the gates shall not be shut: I will go before thee, and make the rough places smooth; I will break in pieces the doors of brass, and cut in sunder the bars of iron; and I will give thee the treasures of darkness, and hidden riches of secret places, that thou mayest know that it is I, Jehovah, who call thee by thy name, even the God of Israel. For Jacob my servant's sake, and Israel my chosen, I have called thee by thy name: I have surnamed thee, though thou hast not known me. I am Jehovah, and there is none else: besides me there is no God. I will gird thee, though thou hast not known me; that they may know from the rising of the sun, and from the west, that there is none besides me: I am Jehovah, and there is none else. I form

the light, and create darkness; I make peace, and create
evil; I am Jehovah, that doeth all these things. (Is. 45.1-7)

Our message is to the church, the members of the
body of Christ. Here in Isaiah 45 we have the heathen
King, Cyrus. Although he was a king just like the other
kings who had oppressed God's people and seemed to
have no value to God, he was nevertheless called by God
as one who was anointed of God. This makes him different from any other heathen king mentioned in the
Bible. He was great and his kingdom was very exten-
sive; but he was also fierce, wicked and heathen. How
could he be called God's anointed, when His word says
(speaking of the holy anointing oil, which represents
the Holy Spirit) that "upon the flesh of man shall it
not be poured" (Ex. 30.32a)? This is because he repre-
sented authority and rule; therefore he was a representative of God. He was a person whom God would use
to carry out His eternal purpose.

In God's hand is the authority over all the nations.
He lifts up nations, and He lays them low. He holds
all the nations in His hands. Here He raised up unbeliev-
ing Cyrus to carry out His purpose. He was behind
Cyrus, about whom and to whom He said, "whose right
hand I have holden, to subdue nations before him, and
I will loose the loins of kings; to open the doors before
him, and the gates shall not be shut: I will go before
thee . . ." Why did God do all this? "For Jacob my servant's sake, and Israel my chosen, I have called thee
by thy name: I have surnamed thee, though thou hast
not known me."

God raised up Babylon to smite Israel for their idolatry. Now He raised up Cyrus to take Israel captive from Babylon and in the fullness of time to say in effect to Israel, "Now go back to your own country." Babylon and Cyrus were given power not for the sake of Babylon or of Cyrus, but for Israel's sake, for the sake of God's people. God meant to use Babylon and Cyrus by raising them up so that they might carry out His purpose in relation to His people.

The purpose of the incident at the tower of Babel was not to cause individuals to speak different languages, but to cause nations to speak different languages. He separated the nations for His own purpose. He has never intended since Babel to have the nations united. It is not in His will and purpose for this dispensation. He lifts up one nation and lays low another for this purpose (in regard to Israel) to be served, and all is in relation to His people. From Adam to Abraham, God's testimony was with individuals. After Abraham, it was not with individuals but with a nation. From then on, nations were raised up and smitten down only as they were of use in regard to God's testimony in His people Israel. Their attitude towards Israel determined whether they were blessed or cursed by God: "I will bless them that bless thee, and him that curseth thee will I curse" (Gen. 12.3a).

But there were times when God could not bless His own people, and these were times when Israel fell into idolatry. Then they were given up to the good pleasure of the nations. Yet whenever they recovered the testimony of God in acknowledging Jehovah as God and that besides Him there was no God, at once God reached out to protect and bless them. They were defeated and destroyed, pillaged and taken captive when they forsook God, for they had lost their testimony. But when a righteous king reigned over Israel and upheld the testimony of God, all their enemies were rendered powerless. All the nations around them were weakened and could not touch them.

God's people were raised up to uphold the testimony of God. Everything which concerned the nations was only in relation to this purpose. Israel committed idolatry to the extent that she defiled the very temple and holy things of God. So God used the nations to chastise her and to punish her. They were to be the means of taking Israel through the fire of afflictions and sufferings in order to cleanse her of idolatry and to recover a pure testimony in her.

In the New Testament period, at the time when Jesus was born, He was born in a time of oppression. We may think this was the worst time for Him to have come; but it was the best time. God did not want the event of the crucifixion of Christ to be shut up and hidden from view in a small country, so He chose a time when the greatest nation-empire on earth, the Imperial Romans, ruled over Israel. Thus the crucifixion of Christ became an affair not exclusively of a tiny country, but of the entire world as then ruled by the Romans. Moreover, it was a time when communications were very open, through the influence and efforts of the Roman Empire. And hence, following the Crucifixion and Resurrection the gospel could easily spread to all nations.

After the crucifixion, resurrection and ascension of

the Lord Jesus, the testimony of God was put into the hands of the church. What was true in the Old Testament time with Israel is now to be true with the church. The nations are raised up and strengthened or cast down and weakened according to their bearing on the testimony as held by the church. Rome was allowed to persecute the church only because in that way there was increase and blessing for the testimony. The hand of God is behind all history and such is related wholly and entirely to the testimony. Because of the Roman persecution there came the scattering of the saints, which meant the carrying of the gospel to all nations under heaven.

Everything in history from then on meant either advance for the church or discipline for the church as some lesson for God's people to learn. All history can only be understood as we read in it the hand of God dealing with His people in regard to His testimony. Our prayers as Christians at this time of world-wide conflict* cannot possibly be so narrowly national, geographical, or even earthly in their definition. Our prayers can only be along this line: "Lord, prosper that nation which stands for Your interests. Advance their cause who advance Your cause. Let them win whose victory You can use. Whoever's victory is of most value to You and to Your testimony, we are for that victory. Whichever opposes Your testimony, we oppose it. Whatever hurts and hinders Your people and Your cause, we are against it.

---

*An allusion to the then recent outbreak of World War Two. —*Translator*

Whatever and whoever helps to bring in the kingdom of Christ, we are for it."

D. THE LORD KNOWS THOSE WHO ARE HIS

> Howbeit the firm foundation of God standeth, having this seal, The Lord knoweth them that are his: and, Let every one that nameth the name of the Lord depart from unrighteousness. Now in a great house there are not only vessels of gold and of silver, but also of wood and of earth; and some unto honor, and some unto dishonor. If a man therefore purge himself from these, he shall be a vessel unto honor, sanctified, meet for the master's use, prepared unto every good work. (2 Tim. 2.19–21)

God has a foundation to His house that cannot be moved. Many of God's children, as they go on, become less and less clear concerning the light which they once had. They grow more and more careless about their actions, life and faith. When you look at them and think of their beginnings, of their fervent, bright and fruitful early years, and then see how they have changed, you feel afraid concerning your own future and wonder what you can hope for. But there is One—even the Lord—who cannot and will not ever change. There is also something else that will not change, and that is the work of God. What He himself does will never be moved. It will never change.

"The Lord knoweth them that are his"—"the firm foundation of God standeth." We may be disappointed in many fellow-Christians; we may wonder who we can really trust, who will really stand and not fall, who is really born again, and who is really true and will go through with the Lord. Nevertheless, let us ever keep in mind that one of the foundations of God's house is: "the Lord knoweth them that are his."

"Now in a great house there are not only vessels of gold and of silver, but also of wood and of earth." Man looks at the use of a vessel, but God does not so look. Instead, He looks at its value. Wooden and earthen vessels in a house are far more useful than gold and silver vessels, but the gold and the silver are more valuable. God's point of view, God's regard, is for value and not for use. He is after preciousness, value and costliness. Much work today is cheap. The office of an elder or of a deacon in a church may be cheap. Preaching may be very cheap. All depends on the vessel, the value of the vessel. Unless you yourself weigh heavy, your words will be cheap. Gold and silver represent that which is from God and of God. Wood and earth represent that which is from man and of man. Gold stands for the nature of God, while silver stands for the redemption of our Lord Jesus.

If you want to be the gold and the silver, you must know the waiting upon the Lord, the looking up to the Lord, praying with believing faith, receiving revelation, laying aside yourself, cutting off the flesh, and dealing with all that is of yourself. This takes time, and it is costly. But value can come to you in no other way. That which is of value is all out from God. All else — what you get from your own thinking or reasoning, what you work out with your own strength — is cheap and valueless.

When we have the cross really dealing with our natural life, that is to say, really dealing with our earthly and lower life, we become something of value. Value is that which comes from a high price having been paid. It has cost us much. But whatever comes out of ourselves, from our natural life, mind and feeling, is that which is cheap and valueless.

E. OUT OF THE ABUNDANCE OF THE HEART THE MOUTH SPEAKS

O my soul, come not thou into their council; unto their assembly, my glory, be not thou united; for in their anger they slew a man, and in their self-will they hocked an ox. Cursed be their anger, for it was fierce; and their wrath, for it was cruel: I will divide them in Jacob, and scatter them in Israel. . . . I have waited for thy salvation, O Jehovah. (Gen. 49.6–7,18)

I said unto the king, Let the king live for ever: Why should not my countenance be sad, when the city, the place of my fathers' sepulchres, lieth waste, and the gates thereof are consumed with fire? Then the king said unto me, For what dost thou make request? So I prayed to the God of heaven. (Neh. 2.3–4)

Now is my soul troubled; and what shall I say? Father, save me from this hour. But for this cause came I unto this hour. Father, glorify thy name. There came therefore a voice out of heaven, saying, I have both glorified it, and will glorify it again. The mulitude therefore, that stood by, and heard it, said that it had thundered: others said, An angel hath spoken to him. Jesus answered and said, This voice hath not come for my sake, but for your sakes. (John 12.27–30)

They exchanged the truth of God for a lie, and worshipped and served the creature rather than the Creator, who is blessed for ever. Amen. (Rom. 1.25)

Whose are the fathers, and of whom is Christ as concerning the flesh, who is over all, God blessed for ever. Amen. (Rom. 9.5)

O the depth of the riches both of the wisdom and the knowledge of God! how unsearchable are his judgments, and his ways past tracing out! For who hath known the mind of the Lord? or who hath been his counsellor? or who hath first given to him, and it shall be recompensed unto him again? For of him, and through him, and unto him, are all things. To him be the glory for ever. Amen. (Rom. 11.33–36)

Grace to you and peace from God our Father and the Lord Jesus Christ. (Eph. 1.2)

Unto him be the glory in the church and in Christ Jesus unto all generations for ever and ever. Amen (Eph. 3.21)

Peace be to the brethren, and love with faith, from God the Father and the Lord Jesus Christ. Grace be with all them that love our Lord Jesus Christ with a love incorruptible. (Eph. 6.23–24)

Whenever God speaks in His word through any man, when He chooses a vessel and this vessel speaks, there is always a sentence or two included in what he says which reveals the man himself. That which he speaks himself, but nevertheless under the control of the Holy Spirit, is a kind of by-play, an exclamation, an outburst, a bit of revelation of himself as to what kind of a man he is. When Jacob was prophesying over his sons, he burst out, "I have waited for thy salvation, O Jehovah." This slips out, as it were, on the side; but it shows us what kind of man Jacob really was. Here we see a man who has been broken by the many dealings of the Lord.

John 12 is one of the very best chapters in the Bible by which we may get acquainted with the Lord Jesus himself. There in verses 27 and 28, He uttered: "Now is my soul troubled; and what shall I say? Father, save me from this hour." "No," He said to himself, "I cannot say *that*, because it was for this reason that I have come unto this hour. No, this is what I will say, 'Father, glorify thy name.'" And immediately upon praying *this*, there came a voice from heaven, saying, "I have both glorified it, and will glorify it again." The cross had not only dealt with all He said to men, it had also dealt with all He said to God. This bit of soliloquy is a sideline set off from the leading textual content of the rest of the chapter. Nonetheless, it distinctively reveals what is within Him.

Out of the abundance of the heart the mouth speaks. Our speaking is sure to betray us. A sentence unpremeditated will slip out during our speech. We cannot hide ourselves.

This was true of the apostle Paul. In Romans 1, he was speaking of the sins of the heathen, how "they exchanged the truth of God for a lie, and worshipped and served the creature rather than the Creator." He could go on no further without putting in a note of praise: "who is blessed for ever. Amen." And then he went on. In Romans 9.5 he did the same thing. He had great sorrow and unceasing pain in his heart for his kinsmen according to the flesh. He spoke of the great privileges they had. But when he came to say, "of whom is Christ as concerning the flesh," he broke in with, "who is over all, God blessed for ever. Amen." There was something in his heart which welled up and could not be suppressed. This shows us how he was a man full of praise and worship.

The same thing happened in Romans 11. He was talking about how God in His great love and wisdom had "shut up all unto disobedience, that he might have mercy upon all" (v. 32). Again, he blurted out his adoration in the very next verse (33): "O the depth of the riches both of the wisdom and the knowledge of God! how unsearchable are his judgments and his ways past tracing out! For who hath known the mind of the Lord? or who hath been his counsellor? or who hath first given to him, and it shall be recompensed unto him again? For of him, and through him, and unto him, are all things. To him be the glory for ever. Amen."

The question today is not about our teaching, for that may be perfectly correct, edifying and splendid; but the question is, what kind of person are you who are speaking? For out of the abundance of the heart the mouth speaks. You cannot hide youself from the hearers. What you really are will slip out in your unguarded words, without your knowing it.

Lord, grant me this grace of not only giving forth the word that You give me, but also of giving forth that which comes from the work of the Holy Spirit within me, that inwrought life out of which and by which I shall be able to minister Christ to others. Amen.

F.   WHAT IS TRUTH?

Ye shall know the truth, and the truth shall make you free. (John 8.32)

Pilate saith unto him, What is truth? (John 18.38a)

Jesus saith unto him, I am the way, and the truth, and the life: no one cometh unto the Father, but by me. (John 14.6)

Oh send out thy light and thy truth; let them lead me. (Ps. 43.3a)

Even the Spirit of truth: whom the world cannot receive; for it beholdeth him not, neither knoweth him: ye know him, for he abideth with you, and shall be in you. (John 14.17)

If so be that ye heard him, and were taught in him, even as truth is in Jesus. (Eph. 4.21)

In whom ye also, having heard the word of the truth, the gospel of your salvation. (Eph. 1.13a)

Sanctify them in the truth: thy word is truth. (John 17.17)

Many of God's children are asking, "What is truth?" Or they are asking, "What is the difference between truth ("chien li" in Chinese) and doctrine ("tao li" in Chinese)?" Let us see what the word of God says. In Hebrew, truth is reality.

In the Gospel of John, two things stand out: (1) grace, which is something that comes because of the cross, a salvation via the cross; and (2) truth, which is also something that comes from the finished work of Christ. Apart from the work of Christ, there is no grace; and it also requires the work of Christ to bring forth truth.

Multitudes accept Christ as the Life and as the Way, but they do not see how He is the Truth. Now, how is He the Truth? By giving up His life, by the sacrifice of His own self, He has redeemed us by His own blood. His blood redeems us—this is a fact, this is truth. In other words, I am what I am because of the blood of Christ. Hence, truth is not a teaching, nor is it a doctrine, but it is what I am before God by Christ's work.

However, when I compare what I am before God by the work of Christ with what I am here in my daily experience, I immediately see that something is wrong. My own experience on earth contradicts the truth of God. What I am in God's sight by virtue of the perfect, finished work of Christ—this is truth. Yet truth is not what I feel myself to be or see myself to be. Which is more real—my own experience or the truth as it is in Christ?

When Christ died on the cross, it was not He, one Person, who died there. On the contrary, God included all of us in the death, resurrection and ascension of Christ. So that the victory of Christ has become our victory; His glory, our glory; and His power, our power.

Suppose we present the work of Christ on the cross to an unsaved person, who then sees it, accepts it and is saved. If someone were to then ask him if he is a Christian, he would say, "Yes, praise the Lord, I am." But in a few months time, circumstances begin to change. Everything seems to go against him. Bad times have come to him. He feels his joy is gone, and his victory fades away. His feelings have all been changed. Now if someone asks him again whether he is saved, he might not know what to say. But, then, what would you say to him? You would say to him, "From the truth point of view, certainly you are saved, even though from the experience point of view there may seem to be no salvation." We must ever look at fact and not at experience. He is saved regardless of his feelings. The more we look at feelings, the less we are delivered. For "ye shall know the truth, and the truth shall make you free." Therefore, let us look at the truth of God and look away from feelings and experience.

Here is another truth of God: I have been included in Christ's death. Until I see that I died in Christ's death, I am not free, I am still enslaved. Christ's death is not simply that of an individual, it is also a corporate death. Many people are bound because they are living in experience. They believe their experience and do not believe the fact or the truth of God, which is the finished work of Christ. As long as we live in our experiences we are going to remain bound by sin and self. But the moment we look at the fact of God we shall be set free. Our feelings have nothing whatsoever to do with it. There can never be deliverance until we behold and believe and live in the truth of God: that when Christ died we too died.

In regard to victory—to overcoming the Enemy— it is precisely the same way. Praying against the Enemy or praying for victory will never work. We have got to look at the finished victory of Christ and live in its reality. It is from that vantage point that we pray downward. We begin with praise for His perfect and accomplished and complete victory and then hold all oppositions beneath that victory: "Ye shall know the truth, and the truth shall make you free."

Many have been seeing their need of light these days, and they are seeking for that light. But upon what does the light of God shine? The light is to shine upon the truth. People may be hearing much about their having died with Christ or in Christ, but nothing has happened to their lives. They remain the same. And why? It is because the light of God has not fallen upon the truth of God, therefore they fail to see the truth. When truth is preached without light, it becomes doctrine. But when truth is preached with light it becomes revelation. When truth is received as doctrine, it gives us a big head. But when truth is received as light or revelation, it becomes life experience.

What is truth? It is Jesus Christ himself; and this includes all His work, since the greater (the Person) includes the lesser (the work). On the one hand, we have the word of truth; while on the other, we have the Spirit of truth. How does God use the Spirit of truth to lead us into the word of truth? It is by having the light of God shine upon the word. Through that one act we are at once brought by the Spirit of truth into a living experience of the reality of that truth. Since Christ is the truth, it means the Spirit of truth brings us at once into Christ, the Truth — that is to say, into all His finished work which has already been accomplished for us. All has been finished; therefore, all that is needed is for us to see the truth of God in the light of God.

G. TASTE THE KINGDOM NOW

As touching those who . . . once . . . tasted the good word of God, and the powers of the age to come. (Heb. 6.4–5)

He said unto them, Verily I say unto you, There is no man that hath left house, or wife, or brethren, or parents, or children, for the kingdom of God's sake, who shall not receive manifold more in this time, and in the world to come eternal life. (Luke 18.29–30)

A new heart also will I give you, and a new spirit will I put within you; and I will take away the stony heart out of your flesh, and I will give you a heart of flesh. And I will put my Spirit within you, and cause you to walk in my statutes, and ye shall keep mine ordinances, and do them. (Ez. 36.26–27)

I saw thrones, and they sat upon them, and judgment was given unto them: and I saw the souls of them that had been beheaded for the testimony of Jesus, and for the word of God, and such as worshipped not the beast, neither his image, and received not the mark upon their forehead and upon their hand; and they lived, and reigned with Christ a thousand years. The rest of the dead lived not until the thousand years should be finished. This is the first resurrection. (Rev. 20.4-5)

In that day there shall be a fountain opened to the house of David and to the inhabitants of Jerusalem, for sin and for uncleanness. (Zech. 13.1)

And it shall be in the last days, saith God, I will pour forth of my Spirit upon all flesh: and your sons and your daughters shall prophesy, and your young men shall see visions, and your old men shall dream dreams. Yea and on my servants and on my handmaidens in those days will I pour forth of my Spirit; and they shall prophesy. (Acts 2.17-18)

If I by the Spirit of God cast out demons, then is the kingdom of God come upon you. (Matt. 12.28)

There remaineth therefore a sabbath rest for the people of God. (Heb. 4.9)

Behold, I have given you authority to tread upon serpents and scorpions, and over all the power of the enemy: and nothing shall in any wise hurt you. (Luke 10.19)

I also say unto thee, that thou art Peter, and upon this rock I will build my church; and the gates of Hades shall not prevail against it. (Matt. 16.18)

The seventh angel sounded; and there followed great voices in heaven, and they said, The kingdom of the world

is become the kingdom of our Lord and of his Christ:
and he shall reign for ever and ever. (Rev. 11.15)

Who delivered us out of the power of darkness, and
translated us into the kingdom of the Son of his love. (Col.
1.13)

This is the age of the church; the next age will be
that of the kingdom. These two ages are close to each
other, but they are quite different. All the fullness of
God—all the completion and fulfillment of the glory
of God—is for the kingdom age and not for the church
age. All the gifts which God has given to the church
are not for this age alone but even more so for the next
age. They are received and developed now for the
ultimate use then in the kingdom. The salvation of the
kingdom is the same salvation as the present one, only
it is received and tasted now. The eternal life now is
the eternal life then; only, that it is given now to prepare
for then.

"A fountain opened . . . for sin and for uncleanness" is the work of Jesus Christ prepared for the
kingdom, but it is now given to a company of people
who are representatives of the kingdom. The Day of
Rest, that is, the rest of God, points to the kingdom;
but a company of people enter into it now. The promises in Ezekiel 36.25–27 are to be fulfilled in the
kingdom, but there is a company of people who enjoy
them in advance.

God says He will not only give the house of Israel
a new heart and a new spirit, He will also put His own
Spirit within them. We know this is to be characteristic

of the kingdom, that all of the house of Israel will have God's Spirit within them. Yet now an advance company, the church, has His Spirit within them today (see Heb. 8.8–12).

The same is true with resurrection. The first resurrection is at the beginning of the Millennium and is for the kingdom; and yet we, the Christians, are the first fruits, the pre-manifestation of that first resurrection: "Faithful is the saying: For if we died with Him, we shall also live with him" (2 Tim. 2.11). So also is it concerning death. At the end of the kingdom age, "death and Hades" will be "cast into the lake of fire. This is the second death, even the lake of fire" (Rev. 20.14). And yet we now can say, "O death, where is thy victory? O death, where is thy sting?" (1 Cor. 15.55) We can say the same thing to Hades because Christ declares: "Upon this rock I will build my church; and the gates of Hades shall not prevail against it."

What we say now can only truly, literally and fully be said of the kingdom age; nevertheless, we are able to say them now. The Lord Jesus declared: "I beheld Satan fallen as lightning from heaven" (Luke 10.18). This will be universally demonstrated in the kingdom age, for then Satan shall be bound for a thousand years; but this, as is made clear in the very next verse, is today a fact and experience to and for the church: "Behold, I have given you authority to tread upon serpents and scorpions, and over all the power of the enemy: and nothing shall in any wise hurt you," continued the Lord Jesus (v. 19). Today we have not yet seen all things put in subjection to Christ, though in the kingdom age we shall so see, both visibly and universally. Nevertheless, we in the age of the church today have already been given the authority won by Him on Calvary's cross.

So we see that although all is for the kingdom, we, the church, enjoy in advance all that is prepared for the kingdom. Hebrews 6.5 states that believers today have "tasted the good word of God, and the powers of the age to come." Praise the Lord! Yet how terrible it is that we have not made use of all this but have left much unused. People may study kingdom teaching, analyze its doctrines, and place each item in its particular niche for the days to come. But this is most useless because all this is nothing but doctrine. The kingdom, with its characteristics, blessings, gifts, power, atmosphere, and all else, is for us *now*. These things are to be tasted *now*. We are to taste the powers of the age to come — *today*. Though we cannot *eat and digest* them all, we are nonetheless most certainly to *taste* them all — and *now*.

How, then, are we going to taste today the powers of the age to come? May God open our eyes to see how the Bible is full of absolute contrasts — out of sin into righteousness, out of death into life, out of sickness into health, out of darkness into light, out of the human into the divine, out of the natural into the spiritual, and so forth. Let us see that God has also delivered us out of this earth, but into what? Is it into heaven? No, the Bible does not say so. It says that we have been delivered out of this earth into the kingdom: our Father God has "delivered us out of the power of darkness, and translated us into the kingdom of the Son of his love."

We need to remember that our ground, our home,

our place is not here, but in the kingdom. We must stand into all the good of the kingdom now. Why is it that when we become Christians everything becomes difficult with relationships, business, and so forth? It is because God wants to show us that our place, our home, our country is no longer on this earth but in the kingdom. We must now live in the kingdom. Unless we are today using the powers God has given us against all the powers of the Enemy, against all the hosts of darkness in the thick of the spiritual battle — resisting, fighting and pressing the battle, we shall be utterly unprepared for the kingdom that is to come in fullness. Like a diver in the sea who has to live by the air from earth even though he is down below the earth, so we have to live down here by the air of the heavenly kingdom; otherwise we shall die. We are to bring the power of the heavenly kingdom to bear upon this earth now. We are not to allow any atmosphere or condition to be present in our home, our business, or in whatever place we are other than the righteousness, the perfection, the pure atmosphere and condition of the kingdom.

Yes, the kingdom is indeed future, but we are to bring it right into wherever we are and into whatever we do *now*. In and through and by the power of God — by the authority of God — which He has given us, we are to bring in the kingdom today wherever we are. "The kingdom of God," declares the Lord Jesus, "is in the midst of you" (Luke 17.21 mg.). Because the King is among us, therefore, wherever we are, there in fact is the kingdom. Yea, "the kingdom of God is within you," for Christ is there in us. Everything in our lives must be a kingdom matter; that is to say — it must be something taken from the kingdom and used now. Consequently, the question comes down to this: Are we taking kingdom power, kingdom blessings, kingdom gifts, kingdom fullness, kingdom position, kingdom viewpoint, kingdom attitude, kingdom everything — and possessing them and using them now? The kingdom is to be tasted now, both in its power, its rule, its glorious fullness, and so forth.

However, all this cannot be experienced alone. For this is not an individual matter, this is a company matter, a matter of the body of Christ. True, we are not to allow anything which is not of the kingdom into our individual surroundings and into our individual places. Yes, individually we are to set our faces towards the kingdom and have and hold everything in relation to the kingdom. But there are many things which we are not able to change or move by ourselves alone. These will have to be changed or moved by the "twos" and "threes" in the church. There are many matters we cannot get through on without the help of the whole church. The greatest loss to the work of God is when the *church* ceases to reign. May God open our eyes to see what is our ministry. If we are facing the kingdom and desiring to bring it right down into the present world, we must pray, we must bind and loose, we must learn to maintain the note and sound of battle. Nothing less than corporate spiritual warfare will carry the day. We need to be prayer-warriors, yet not praying alone but praying together. If, however, we ourselves individually are not living in and for the kingdom, we shall most certainly be defeated, we being perfectly useless to God. May God be gracious to us.

PART TWO

PULLED-OUT SHEAVES*

*See Ruth 2.15–16

1 | Watch and be Sober*

On that day there came to him Sadducees, they that say that there is no resurrection: and they asked him saying, Teacher, Moses said, If a man die, having no children, his brother shall marry his wife, and raise up seed unto his brother. Now there were with us seven brethren: and the first married and deceased, and having no seed left his wife unto his brother; in like manner the second also, and the third, unto the seventh. And after them all, the woman died. In the resurrection therefore whose wife shall she be of the seven? for they all had her. But Jesus answered and said unto them, Ye do err, not knowing the scriptures, nor the power of God. (Matt. 22.23–29)

So then let us not sleep, as do the rest, but let us watch and be sober. (1 Thess. 5.6)

A group of Sadducees, who did not believe in resur-

---

*Translated and published in English for the first time.—*Translator*

rection, came and asked the Lord Jesus a question. To us the question they put to Him was indeed a most peculiar question and one that is seldom met. There were seven brothers in one place who married the same woman one after another. They all died without leaving a child. This would appear to be highly fictitious. So that these Sadducees were obviously intent upon using this question to tempt the Lord Jesus and to refute the belief in resurrection. Yet, as we see in the Bible, their fabricated story did not ruffle the Lord one whit. Instead, He calmly struck back, saying, "Ye do err, not knowing the scriptures, nor the power of God." The Lord Jesus declared that they were wrong. Both their insinuation and their question were wrong. Why did they ask such a strange question fabricated out of their fanciful imagination? For what reason did they refuse to believe in resurrection? Why were they wrong? Let us see that He pointed out clearly that all this was due to their not knowing the Scriptures nor the power of God.

Now we do not intend to explain this passage of Scripture. We only desire to derive an important principle out of this portion of God's word. Though this speaks of the erring of the Sadducees, it also tells of the knowledge which a Christian ought to possess. A Christian is a believer in the Lord Jesus, but he is still subject to error. He may be wrong without even knowing it. The two main explanations for such a condition to be able to exist are: first, a not knowing the Scriptures, and second, a not knowing the power of God. If we expect to walk well on the spiritual path, to serve well in the Lord's work, or to be in the will of God in our managing church affairs, in expounding the Scriptures, and in our daily living, we must know the Scriptures, and we must also know the power of God.

"Every scripture inspired of God is also profitable for teaching, for reproof, for correction, for instruction which is in righteousness: that the man of God may be complete, furnished completely unto every good work" (2 Tim. 3.16-17). No good Christian who desires to please the Lord is unfamiliar with the word of God. What God speaks to men today is based on what He has spoken before in the Scriptures. We may say that the Scriptures have already told us what is the will and mind of God and what are the things that please or displease Him. "Thy word is a lamp unto my feet, and light unto my path" (Ps. 119.105).

As we walk on the spiritual pathway, we need light to keep us from missing the right direction or from falling. The word of God is the lamp to our feet and the light on our path. In order to avoid error in our spiritual journey, we must follow the Scriptures. In the Book of Psalms, it is further written: "Thy word have I laid up in my heart, that I might not sin against thee" (Ps. 119.11). There is only one way for us to be those who do not sin against the Lord, and that is, to lay up the word of the Lord in our heart richly. If a child of God will spend time in reading the Bible well, taking it as his sole signpost and studying it with a God-fearing heart, he will be saved from falling into destructive errors of thought and conduct.

Today we have the Holy Spirit indwelling us as well as the Scriptures before us. According to the New Covenant, God has put His law within us. This is the law of the Spirit of life mentioned in Romans 8.2 (also cf. Heb. 8.10). This is also the Anointing which teaches us in all things as explained in 1 John 2.27 (also cf. Heb. 8.10-11). If we do not quench the Spirit but are willing to learn to submit to the teaching of the inner anointing, we will be kept from falling into errors. The reason why God's children make so many errors in their spiritual pursuit is because of not knowing the Scriptures and the power of God.

There were people in the past who paid all their attention to signs and wonders. They talked about nothing else except these in every place, and many seemed to love hearing these things. In addition, there were people who talked all the time about visions and dreams. They had seen so many visions and dreams that they taught them as though they themselves were the great prophets and great apostles raised up by God. Sometimes these people did exhibit some supernatural power. They could reveal hidden things of men. They therefore attracted many immature believers to follow after them, inquiring of them as though these teachers were great prophets indeed. There were still other people who prayed strange prayers. They repeated a monotonous phrase hundreds of times. There were even people who claimed that the Lord Jesus had already come the second time or that He would come at a certain day in a certain month and year. Let us realize, however, that if we search the Scriptures carefully, we will discover that all these above situations are questionable. Let us look at several of them separately.

Concerning Signs and Wonders

We believe in signs and wonders. We believe that the Lord Jesus heals the sick and casts out demons. He is the Son of God, so it is quite natural for Him to perform miracles. He is the Creator of the universe; to Him, healing the sick and casting out demons are actually two insignificant matters. However, we see from the Bible that whenever people came to tempt Him and ask for a sign, He never complied with their requests (see Matt. 16.1–4). He did not want people to believe Him after they had seen Him performing wonders (cf. John 4.48). While He was on earth, He often commanded people whom He had healed not to broadcast these events (see, e.g., Matt. 8.4; Mark 5.43 — "he charged them *much* that no man should know this"; 7.36). And why? Because our Lord did not wish to have people follow Him simply out of curiosity alone. Even though many believed Him, beholding the signs which He did, He nonetheless did not trust himself to them "because he knew what was in man" (see John 2.23–25). The five thousand mentioned in John 6 eventually left Him after they had witnessed the multiplication of the loaves and fishes which they had eaten. For the one who *truly* knows the Lord, knows Him not by external signs and wonders but by the word of God and the revelation of the Holy Spirit.

We believe the demons were subject to the seventy disciples (Luke 10.17). We also believe Peter, John, Stephen and Paul all performed wonders, healed the sick, and cast out demons (see Acts 3.2–8; 6.8; 9.36–41; 14.8–18; 16.16–18; 28.1–6). We believe as well the word in Mark 16.17 which states: "these signs shall accompany them that believe." But as understood from the Scriptural viewpoint we should not use signs and wonders, healing and exorcising, to attract and collect people. For these things are not the center of salvation, and hence they should not occupy too big a place. The name of the Lord is alone worthy to be exalted.

It is thus clear that people who seek and talk of nothing but signs and wonders act unscripturally. These people may easily be deceived by Satan, because false prophets and false Christs do also show great signs and wonders (see Matt. 24.24; Mark 13.22; 2 Thess. 2.9–12). We need to have a right knowledge of the power of God, but never treat signs and wonders with mere curiosity.

Concerning Visions and Dreams

It is true that in the Old Testament time God sometimes taught His people through visions and dreams, though these were not as frequent as we might think. In the New Testament period, especially after the coming of the Holy Spirit, there are still visions and dreams; but each occurrence has its specific cause. For during the age of the New Testament, with the Holy Spirit already indwelling us, God normally will teach us all things by the Anointing in us. On the one hand God wants us to base everything in our lives on the word of the Scriptures, and on the other hand to know His mind through the sensing of inner life.

It is true that in the New Testament there are a few incidents of visions and dreams. One such occasion was when Peter, as he was sleeping on the housetop of

Simon the tanner in Joppa, saw a great sheet descending, wherein were all manner of four-footed beasts and creeping things of the earth and birds of the air (see Acts 10.9–12). Why did the Lord give Peter this vision? It was because Peter at that time had a very deep prejudice against the Gentiles. So the Lord used a vision to break his prejudice, to open the way of the gospel to the Gentiles. Paul also saw visions a few times. Twice God used them to comfort and strengthen him in times of distress (Acts 18.9–10; 27.23–24).

We do acknowledge that visions and dreams have their place in the Scriptures; nevertheless, they cannot be taken as our only guidance. Having received visions and dreams, we need to see if they agree with the word of the Bible, the teaching of the inner Anointing and the ordering of outward circumstances. After Peter saw the vision in Joppa, he received immediate confirmation from the circumstances, for the messengers sent by Cornelius arrived at his place. Visions and dreams are dependable, therefore, only if they themselves are meaningful and purposeful as well as in harmony with the word of the Bible, the teaching of the Anointing and the confirmation of the circumstances.

Let us be aware, however, that in the New Testament time, visions and dreams are not the regular way God uses to guide people. Even if visions and dreams have been given, their contents are not necessarily revealed. Paul, for example, had the experience of the third heaven, yet he did not divulge it until fourteen years later—and under compulsion at that! (2 Cor. 12.1–6) If anyone claims to have seen visions and dreams frequently, such a person possibly has some problem with his mind.

We ought to know that many sudden thoughts are often injected into the human mind from outside by evil spirits. A believer may have lightning thoughts coming to his mind, causing him to understand, comprehend, or discover some peculiar matters or suggestions for him to act upon. These thoughts should be rejected because they do not come from the Holy Spirit.

Evil spirits will not only inject thoughts into a believer's mind, they will also project all kinds of imaginary pictures into the mind of the believer as well. Some are beautiful and pleasing to the believer; some are dirty and hated by the believer's conscience. Notwithstanding whether good or bad, pleasant or hateful, the believer has been deceived if he has no power to forbid such imaginary pictures to remain in his mind.

A dream can be natural or supernatural. It can come from God; it can also come from the demons. Apart from those which are induced by one's own physiological or psychological state or condition, the rest are all supernatural in source. A believer who suffers a nervous breakdown through pressure or sickness and who is not familiar with the Scriptures may have his mind open to the assaults of evil spirits. Thus he may dream many dreams. We know for sure that the dreams which come from God give peace and steadfastness as well as are rational and purposeful; while those which come from evil spirits are strange, vain, absurd and foolish, thus causing people to lose their reasoning.

Let us not consider all visions and dreams as good. Remember that many of these phenomena do not come from God. They must not be accepted; instead, they should be rejected. Thus, you will be delivered from being deceived.

Due to a psychological disorder or to deception of evil spirits some people may create imaginations in their minds. These are often the most arrogant and subjective of all men. They frequently imagine themselves as great prophets or great apostles raised up by God. We ought to know that all who are under deception by evil spirits are people who are so self-confident that they will not easily accept others' advice, nor will they trust in the feelings of other brothers and sisters.

What is worse, however, and because of certain supernatural elements in these visions and dreams, these visionaries and dreamers may easily attract those ignorant, immature and curious believers to follow them. They consider themselves to be great prophets and apostles raised up by God, and these ignorant and immature believers will regard them as such. Some are even inquired of as though they were God himself. All this is unscriptural.

From the New Testament viewpoint, there are only prophets of the church; God never allows His children to be prophets of individuals. For under the New Covenant, the law of God is no longer inscribed on outward stone tablets, but rather is written upon our hearts (see Heb. 8.10). All who have the life of God have the ability to know the mind of God. Under the New Covenant, God does not allow anyone to be a prophet to an individual — that is to say, to know the will of God for another individual believer. Hence we need to ask God to deliver us from a curious mind, lest we fall into deception.

Concerning the Matter of the Coming of the Lord Jesus

We believe in the second coming of the Lord Jesus. This is part of our basic faith. Yet the Bible never tells us the day of the coming of our Lord: "of that day and hour knoweth no one, not even the angels of heaven, neither the Son, but the Father only" (Matt. 24.36); also, "Jesus answered and said unto them, Take heed that no man lead you astray. For many shall come in my name, saying, I am the Christ; and shall lead many astray" (Matt. 24.4–5); and again, "if any man shall say unto you, Lo, here is the Christ, or, Here; believe it not. For there shall arise false Christs, and false prophets, and shall show great signs and wonders; so as to lead astray, if possible, even the elect. . . . If therefore they shall say unto you, Behold, he is in the wilderness; go not forth: Behold, he is in the inner chambers; believe it not" (Matt. 24.23–26); and finally, "Watch therefore, for ye know not the day nor the hour" (Matt. 25.13).

We have the same word in Mark 13. Our Lord clearly told His disciples: "Take heed that no man lead you astray. Many shall come in my name, saying, I am he; and shall lead many astray" (vv.5–6); "if any man shall say unto you, Lo, here is the Christ; or, Lo, there; believe it not: for there shall arise false Christs and false prophets, and shall show signs and wonders, that they may lead astray, if possible, the elect. But take ye heed: behold, I have told you all things beforehand" (vv.

21–23); and finally, "of that day or that hour knoweth no none, not even the angels in heaven, neither the Son, but the Father. Take ye heed, watch and pray: for ye know not when the time is" (vv.32–33).

Paul, too, warned in 2 Thessalonians 2: "to the end that ye be not quickly shaken from your mind, nor yet be troubled, either by spirit, or by word, or by epistle as from us, as that the day of the Lord is just at hand" (v.2); for "even he [the man of sin], whose coming is according to the working of Satan with all power and signs and lying wonders" (v.9).

When the Lord Jesus mentioned His coming again to the disciples, He warned them, saying: "Watch." This word is repeated three times in Mark 13.33–7. Therefore, concerning the second coming of our Lord, we should be sober, watch, pray, and wait. We should be prepared daily to meet our Lord. We ought to wait for our Lord by constantly watching and praying. The Bible does not permit us to be so foolish as to calculate the day and hour of the coming of the Lord Jesus. We must be watchful lest we be deceived if any should come and declare that the Lord Jesus will come in a certain month and on a certain day.

Concerning Repeating One Word in Prayer

In praying, some people repeat over and over again such words as: "Praise the Lord, praise the Lord" or "Hallelujah, hallelujah," and so forth. By repeating one word or sentence aloud in prayer, it proves in the end to be able to create a blank mind, thus possibly causing strange things to happen. People can be deceived by evil spirits into thinking that they are filled with the Holy Spirit. The preacher tells us, "Be not rash with your mouth, and let not thy heart be hasty to utter anything before God" (Eccl. 5.2a). Our Lord also teaches us not to use vain repetitions (see Matt. 6.7). Prayer is not a reciting of the Scriptures, nor is it the repeating of one word or phrase. Prayer is making our requests known to God (see Phil. 4.6). The Bible also instructs us to be of peace and not of confusion: "Let all things be done decently and in order" (1 Cor. 14.40).

Therefore, let us watch and pray with trembling. Do not be overly self-confident. Learn to be led by the in-dwelling Holy Spirit; listen well to the teaching of the Anointing. At the same time, know the Scriptures. Reject all which disagrees with God's word. Let us remember that when our Lord Jesus was tempted in the wilderness, He used the word of God in overcoming Satan's temptations. We should spend time in reading the Bible so as to store the word of God richly in our hearts. Then shall we be saved from many strange doctrines.

We really thank God, for He gives to the church two great treasures: one is the Bible, the other is the Holy Spirit. We will not err if we truly follow the Bible and the Holy Spirit. Oh, how easily we err, how prone we are to be deceived. Let us remember well the words of Paul in 1 Thessalonians 5.6: "So then let us not sleep, as do the rest, but let us watch and be sober." Unless we search the Scriptures and take the Bible as the lamp to our feet and the light to our path, unless we submit to the authority of the Holy Spirit with fear and trembling, watching and praying constantly, being fearful lest we fall into error, we are indeed too pitiful, we are indeed too much in darkness. May we prostrate ourselves at the Lord's feet, beseeching Him to enlighten us and to keep us, to give us a firm desire to please Him at any cost.

We must reject whatever is unscriptural and keep whatever is according to the Scriptures. At the same time, we must submit ourselves to the authority of the Holy Spirit, not daring to have our own opinions and ideas in instructing men nor serving God according to what pleases our flesh. May God be gracious to His church and keep His church pure and without blemish.

2 | How Is Life Matured?*

> Moab hath been at ease from his youth, and he hath settled on his lees, and hath not been emptied from vessel to vessel, neither hath he gone into captivity: therefore his taste remaineth in him, and his scent is not changed. (Jer. 48.11)

Any kind of fruit needs time to ripen. The young people may acquire an enlarged head, but they cannot be instantly matured. Some people, however, take too long a time to mature. When we forgive people two, three, or up to five times, our hands begin to tremble. The problem lies in capacity. Maturity is having our capacity expanded by God within a reasonable amount of time. No one can reach maturity without being expanded by the hand of God. We may remit a debt of five dollars, but we cannot remit a debt of five thou-

---

*Never before published in any language.—*Translator*

sand dollars. God is willing to spend time on us. He allows us to suffer things unbearable once and again in order to expand our capacity.

The lives of many believers are too tranquil and comfortable. Because they have never been dealt with, therefore their capacity remains small. They are like Moab whose original scent has not changed. They have not been emptied from vessel to vessel. How sad that after some five years, the capacity of many children of God stays unenlarged. They will lose their temper just as badly today over having their dress made wet by a glass of spilled water as they did ten years before.

The difference between an unripe and a ripe fruit lies in their taste. The taste of an unripe fruit is sour and bitter, while that of the ripe one is sweet. Madame Guyon was a teacher of the old because of her rich experience; yet she was a friend to little children because of her sweetness. The life of a Christian is something natural. It is not like some bananas which are ripened artificially.

"I buffet my body," observed Paul, "and bring it into bondage" (1 Cor. 9.27a). Yet on the other hand, our Lord said this: "The Son of man came eating and drinking" (Matt. 11.19a). Some can neither eat nor drink, for the moment they do so their original scent will be exposed. The lilies grow naturally without effort. The birds develop their feathers spontaneously. That which is manufactured and prepared may teach you to be saints among men, but it cannot make you Christians. We need to have the marks of the cross upon us, yet these are not put there by self-effort. Paul had no self-inflicted marks (cf. Gal. 6.17). For though his letters were weighty and strong, his bodily presence was weak (see 2 Cor. 10.10).

We may *delay* the growth of the life of God's Son in us, but we have no way of *accelerating* it. Because of this, it is of utmost importance that we accept the ordering of God. His ordering is seen in the discipline of the Holy Spirit. "Are not two sparrows sold for a penny? and not one of them shall fall on the ground without your Father" (Matt. 10.29). "Are not five sparrows sold for two pence? and not one of them is forgotten in the sight of God" (Luke 12.6). Arithmetically speaking, two pence should buy four sparrows. There is here an extra sparrow which is casually added. Even this extra sparrow is not forgotten by the heavenly Father. How much more will we be cared for as children of God.

Therefore, let us not try our best to escape that which God has ordained. In escaping we miss the ordering of God, thus missing an opportunity to be expanded. The time for maturity will be prolonged, and the lesson will have to be relearned in order for us to be matured. It is like fulfilling the required amount of credits in school. If less credits are taken one year, more must be taken the next. Even after ten years, the required amount must be accumulated.

Accept the discipline of the Holy Spirit. Let Him enlarge your capacity. A believer will not be the same after he has suffered. If he is not expanded, he will become harder. For this reason, when he undergoes suffering, he should remember that maturity is the sum total of the disciplines of the Holy Spirit. We tend to see the maturity of a person but fail to see the accumulation of the discipline of the Holy Spirit in that person.

3 | A Workman Who Need Not Be Ashamed*

Give diligence to present thyself approved unto God, a workman that needeth not to be ashamed, handling aright the word of truth. (2 Tim. 2.15)

Man Must Be Right; Life Is More Essential

We do not work for work's sake, we work according to the will of God. We cannot live in the work; rather, we must live in the life of Christ.

---

*What appears below is the record of a very precious talk which took place between the author and some of his fellow-workers sometime around the year 1950 or 1951 shortly before his arrest and subsequent imprisonment for 20 years on account of his faith. This extant record constitutes, as it were, "a brand plucked out of the fire" (Zech. 3.2), because the text of it had been miraculously preserved for nearly 30 years before finally, after passing through many hands and traversing the seas, it reached the hands of the Publishers. May this unusual heart-to-heart talk stir a responsive chord in all our hearts, even as "deep calleth unto deep" (Ps. 42.7).—*Translator*

The foundation of our work is life, and the way of the work is the cross. Unless a thing is done in life and has undergone the dealings of the cross, it cannot be reckoned as work. Hence, it behooves us not to stress the outer work more than the inner life of Christ. Real service, providing true supply, must be done in life.

God pays attention to the person more than anything else. If the person is not right, none of his works will be right. To an unreliable man, the word "work" is not even in his vocabulary. But to the right man, there is no fear of having no work to do.

For this reason we do not cast out demons merely for the sake of casting out demons, nor do we preach the gospel simply for the sake of preaching the gospel. Everything done is for God's sake. When God moves us, we move. When He is still, we keep still. We cannot depart from God and be active in external work.

One whose life is rich and strong has no fear of not working. The greater one's ministry is, the wider his service will be. For service is based on a person's ministry.

I once saw a doctor who kept very busy even after his retirement. Many still went to consult him. Where there is sugar, there will be ants who need no special invitation.

Before we can talk about work, we must first be touched and broken by the Lord, and first be brought by Him to a right condition.

How we must first receive grace. May there be a beginning in our lives, when whatever is of the flesh and of man, be it opinion, method or idea, is cast aside.

The problem today lies not in teaching, for teaching

cannot solve any difficulty. What is required is practical learning and exercise, the dealing with self in many areas of failure.

Hence, we need to be more humble, more yielding and more dying to self. We must not live in ourselves, but instead allow God to live in us.

The cross is absolutely essential, because without death there can be no life. The measure of life is based on the degree of death. The apostle Paul observed this: "always bearing about in the body the dying of Jesus, that the life also of Jesus may be manifested in our body. For we who live are always delivered unto death for Jesus' sake, that the life also of Jesus may be manifested in our mortal flesh. So then death worketh in us, but life in you" (2 Cor. 4.10–12). He who rejects the cross is never able to live out life. One must be broken, since brokenness is the way of the release of the spirit. The breaking of the man and the releasing of the spirit is a most fundamental lesson.*

The heart of the matter is therefore man. The principal dealing which we tried to emphasize at Kuling**

---

*The author has devoted an entire volume to this very important lesson of the Christian life. Please consult Watchman Nee, *The Release of the Spirit*, 2nd Edition (Cloverdale, Indiana: Ministry of Life, 1976). Originally translated and published in English, 1965. —*Translator*

**The mountain site near Foochow in Fukien Province, South China, for the Training Sessions held in 1948 and 1949 for fellow-workers. See footnote, first page, next chapter, for more information on the Kuling Conferences.—*Translator*

was to make man right. Some people did not experience much change after the Kuling training, whereas some others showed great change. The reason is because some who received only the teaching at Kuling had not really gotten hold of the spiritual reality whereas others did grasp hold of the real thing.

It is of prime importance that the man be right. He must receive grace and be brought into a right condition.

The Church and Service

Today is an extraordinary time. Since there will not be a perfect church on earth, God is raising up overcomers to be the outlet of heaven in accomplishing His purpose.

Today's situation is rather complicated, and God's work in various places is not regimented. Each place has its special feature, thus manifesting the abundant glory of the work of God.

What was in the past cannot be copied, and what was done abroad must not be duplicated. We need to live in revelation.

With God's revelation we can work; without God's revelation we must desist from working. Work itself is rather simple; the difficulty lies with man. Having the right man, there is no fear of having no work from God, for even in the most arduous environment there will always be work if the man is right. "To obey is better than sacrifice" (1 Sam. 15.22b). We should not be attentive to work only and overlook obedience and hearkening.

The current time is especially confusing. Hence we especially need light lest we go astray.

Follow the current of the Holy Spirit and proceed straight forward. Do not mind negative things. Some people may falter, others may fall away, but we must go on.

In spiritual matters do not be afraid of people's opposition. If things are of God, eventually people will acknowledge them to be right.

The way of the church is in Christ, for He is the Way. It lies not in a view or method outside of Christ. The church is not something of the outward man; it is the Christ that is in man. And that is beyond the touch of the world.

People may touch the visible church on earth and even break it, but who can touch and break things that are invisible? Consequently, let us not strongly demand the proper outward form; rather, let us concentrate on the life of Christ within. If a few will seek for testimony by life with one accord, they will bring heaven down upon this earth.

The service God seeks is to supply Christ. It is to profit people with the supply of life. It therefore requires that first of all those who serve be filled with Christ within themselves.

The church ought not to be filled with teachings, but it should be filled with Christ, with the life of Christ. Without the outflow of the life of Christ from within, service is entirely out of the question.

In the church, special attention should be paid to the supply of life in order to lead people into touch with the life of Christ and to live therein. Do not stress only baptism, head-covering, breaking of bread, and so forth. Doctrine is always limited, whereas life is unlimited. It is quite simple to get people to submit to a teaching; it is more useful, however, to cause people to be joined to life and to live by that life. At each attempt to work consider whether or not there is something worth supplying to people. First be connected with the fountain of living water, or else you can only supply others with a bottle of water.

The Christ life is living. It tends to grow and expand. It is not something dead. After a person has received life, you will notice that the spiritual condition in that one will undergo constant changes. Such growth is not the result of outward teaching; rather, it is the maturing and expanding of the inner life, that all may see the person's progress.

What we must center on is life. So-called revival is useless; sometimes it is even harmful. This is because people's appetite for hearing good teaching is so whipped up that they lose their interest in listening to the preaching of the local brothers.

The principle governing work is from inside to outside, and from a few to the many. First gain a few persons, and then through these few gain many more. Work becomes very difficult if there is mutual suspicion instead of one accord. Work is easy when there is harmony within.

There is a principle laid out in the Bible which makes clear that workmen are sent out in twos or more, with there being one mind and proper coordination among them. For example, Peter and John were sent to Samaria; Paul and Barnabas went out together; later on, Paul, Silas, Timothy, Titus and others worked in beautiful coordination. All manifested the strength of perfect accord. It is therefore our hope that God will raise up in every locality people who are truly of one mind. The judgment of two is more accurate than that of one. Words spoken by two are more comprehensive than those of one person. One may be the leader, the other the associate. One speaks with authority, while the other serves as an exemplar of submission. With the harmonious coordination of the two persons the measure of strength will be greatly increased.

The state or condition of a local assembly is not governed by its smallness or largeness but by the spiritual content and heavenly condition within it. If the heavenly atmosphere is good, and no matter however small or big the assembly may be, all is well. But if its spiritual condition is bad, its being small or big will not be acceptable one way or the other. We must thus pay more attention to spiritual content.

When I heard of the sudden increase of thousands being added to a local assembly, I was somewhat apprehensive for them. How and with what are we going to supply these many people? If its spiritual content is inadequate, then the more people there are and the more work there is, the greater will be the difficulty.

In a workers meeting, do not only discuss church matters and arrange works, but let each one tell of his own spiritual condition. A person first needs to receive grace and deliverance from God, and then he can talk about work. Let us always remember that the dealing of the man is far more important than the dealing with affairs.

God has His special work as well as His general work. Preaching the gospel, saving souls, and so forth —these are general works. And of course, these are good. But there is also a special work which is done on a few people so that they may have the specific ministry of touching the mind of God and accomplishing the work of God.

Each person has his particular problem. Some may have a problem with money; some, with the opposite sex; some, with pride; some, with subjectivity; etc. etc. Learn to deal with the special difficulty in each life. Help that person to see his problem through positive, negative and various other approaches.

In situations where the gospel work is blessed, ask for more revelation and more workmen approved of God.

In places where people frequently fast in order to cast out demons, be alert to the wiles of the Enemy. Do not be drawn along by Satan, lest we waste our time and energy. We must be clear about the will of God.

How to Train the Young People

Do not be afraid if young people fail. Fear lest they have no practical learning of lessons.

Do not let the young people have only doctrinal instruction, but help them to have practical dealings. Teach them to learn from having dealings with God through various circumstances.

It is useless for young people to have only zeal; they must have practical dealings and learn lessons in life.

It is possible to start serving with gifts, but gradually to shift to serving with life.

Do not make excessive demands upon young people that they must serve with life, because this is next to impossible. Such kind of service requires time and practical experiences. They may begin to serve with gifts, though they should not be satisfied with such service. They must seek to attain to service with life.

In the training of young people, the emphasis should be on life. Make life the chief objective. Concentrate especially on a few promising ones by patiently cultivating them to become good materials for the Lord's work. Discover the main problem in each life and help them to deal seriously with it.

The receptive power of a young believer is very strong. Therefore, at the outset, care should be taken that nothing wrong is accepted. Once something wrong is received, it is hard to change it.

How could we help a young sister who served well before marriage but finds herself so entangled with domestic affairs after marriage that she is no longer free to serve? She is very anxious about this situation. How are we going to help her? Should we encourage her to quarrel with her folks daily and abdicate her domestic duties in order to go out and serve? This is definitely not the way. Instead, help her to fulfill all her domestic duties well and learn under discipline, so that she may accumulate rich reserves for better service in the future.

It is recorded in the Scriptures: "Then shall two men be in the field; one is taken, and one is left: two women shall be grinding at the mill; one is taken, and one is left" (Matt. 24.40–41); also, "In that night there shall be two men on one bed; the one shall be taken, and the other shall be left" (Luke 17.34). The ones taken are not taken because they happen at that moment to be reading the Bible, praying, attending a meeting, or serving; rather, they are taken because of the way they live before God. The ones left are left because their life condition before God is not right. What is essential is how they live before God and not what they are doing at that particular time. So the young people must be trained to live under God-ordained environments and to have practical dealings so that they may make progress in spiritual life. This is most vital.

Be Attentive to a Worker's Life

Many look only at work and overlook the worker. They consider what work to do and how to do it, but they are not concerned with the worker himself. In God's eyes, the worker is far more important than the work. Can there be work without the workman? Yet how sad that few really pay any attention to the daily life of the worker.

During days gone by, God had really performed great miracles among us. However, many knew only the miracles of sicknesses being healed and demons being cast out; they failed to see the greater miracles which happened in the lives of those who passed through great trials and in their families. When the church was in tribulation, the number of those who suffered was great, and greater still was the number of their family members who likewise suffered. Their situations were extremely difficult. Not only did the world despise them, even the brothers and sisters stood far from them. At chance encounters on the street and elsewhere, they were not even given a glance of recognition. But God has not forsaken them. He did not allow them to die of hunger, He instead brought them through these trials. Are those not greater miracles?

In Moses' leading the children of Israel out of Egypt, many only see the great wonder of crossing the Red Sea. Actually, the greater wonder lies in the fact that for forty years God fed millions of people in the wilderness, who neither tilled nor planted but were kept alive without hunger or lack of anything.

It is important to pay attention to the need of the worker. One must not only have his own need met but also see that others may live too.

Naturally, the spiritual condition of a worker is of great importance. If a worker is not right, the work he does cannot be right. God looks at what kind of person you are. He notices what you *are* more than what you *do*.

Accept the Dealings of the Cross

"I John, your brother and partaker with you in the tribulation and kingdom and patience which are in Jesus" (Rev. 1.9). Tribulation and kingdom and patience are not matters of doctrine but are practical matters. Who is ever void of feeling when he passes through tribulation? In tribulation, one has to endure day after day and year after year until the time is fulfilled. The kingdom is related to authority. One must first be sub-

ject to God's authority and be an obedient person
before authority can pass out through him. How can
those who are disobedient to God go out to cast out
demons? How can they cause the demons to be subject to them?

If a person in official authority and position has
spiritual authority as well (which means his having the
reality of life, with inner anointing as well as outward
supplying), then it is quite natural for people to submit to him. But if what he possesses is only positional
authority without the reality of spiritual life, it creates
a hardship for people ever to submit. Nevertheless, people still need to learn to submit in order to cultivate
the character of submission and become obedient
people.

A brother once asked me, "How should I seek for
the crown of glory?" My answer was, "Do not seek it,
for seeking is futile. Accept the thorny crown today, and
the crown of glory will be yours in the future. But reject the thorny crown today, and you will not have the
crown of glory in the future even though you seek after
it."

Today there is no other way but that of the cross.
The chief lesson today is to take up the cross daily and
die daily. Without death there can be no resurrection;
without suffering there can be no glory.

Death is to sever relationship with self. It is a matter
of growing dead to self and dead to self-consciousness.
God allows many things to come our way with the purpose in view of letting us die to self. The living way
lies in the path of disregarding personal glory or shame,
being willing to lose face, and totally submitting to the
environment that God has ordered.

4 | The Final Word*

According to human estimate, the convening of this Training Session was an impossible attempt. My health has been poor, the environment has been difficult, and finance has been uncertain. It would appear as though the Lord did not want us to have it. Even when we began, we did not know whether we could meet even for a single week. But God has been merciful to us and has brought us to this day [the very last day of the

---

*This final word of exhortation, which in part appears prophetic in nature, was addressed to those 100 or so fellow-workers from near and far who were present at the Second Training Session that had begun in the spring of 1949 on Mount Kuling just outside Foochow, southern China, but which, for security reasons stemming from the civil war that was even then raging nearby between the Chinese Nationalist and Communist troops, had shortly afterwards been moved down to the city below where it safely continued several months more till its conclusion in August. As it turned out, this was to be the last of such Training Conferences ever to be held at Kuling. The First Training Session conducted by the author had been held on Mount Kuling the previous year (1948) for four months beginning in June.—*Translator*

months-long Training Session]. Daily we have had problems, but the Lord has led us through all.

For many years the Lord had called me to serve those who serve Him. In the early days I had tried to prepare such a place for training in the vicinity of Shanghai. Unfortunately, the church was not sympathetic, and my fellow-workers failed to see the need. By myself I built two houses in Tsun-Ru.* The electricity was installed on August 12, 1937, and the war** broke out the next day, August 13th. The brother who watched the buildings left first. The neighboring houses were all kept intact; only our buildings were completely razed.

After I returned from England in 1939, I continued my special ministry by renting some houses in Yu Hwa Villas and Yu Yuen Road† for fellow-workers to live in. Again I was not able to do what I would have liked to do. Some who received the training returned home without learning much, and yet they exhibited great pride.

The way of the Lord is now clear. Perhaps in the days of Tsun-Ru my discipline was insufficient, my learning incomplete, and my words inadequate. Since 1943 I had been preparing Kuling, and this is now the Second Training Session. The ministry which God has

---

*A district in the outskirts of Shanghai.—*Translator*

**A reference to the Sino-Japanese War (1937–45) whose hostilities only ceased with the Japanese surrender to the Allies at the end of World War Two (1939–45).—*Translator*

†All in Shanghai.—*Translator*

given me is to serve all who administer the churches and all who minister God's word. My ministry is to help those who are on the way to the New Jerusalem to walk faster, to make the good even better, not a ministry to help change the bad to good.

In case you fail after you leave here, you can never say afterwards that you did not know the way, nor can you ever say afterwards you have never seen nor sensed this way. Perhaps all through your lives you have never until now met a person who has spoken so frankly to you. Never in my life before have I ever done such a thing. For over twenty years I have not reprimanded any brother. Now I have not held back anything. I have done my duty.

In church history, God has raised up many ministers of the Word. This time I seem to have done a foolish thing, for I have told you my ministry. I have given you myself as well as my teaching. I believe that in these last hours the Lord will be expressed through you. As you return home, you know on the one hand what brotherly love is, and on the other hand what authority is. The demand on you is going to be great, perhaps the greatest demand you will ever meet in all your lives. Unless you put your all on the altar, you will never make it. By the grace of God, may you all be able to respond, "I am willing." In the two thousand years of church history, today especially calls for total commitment. As you go back, remember from whom you have learned. Whether or not the Lord has His way will depend on how you behave. Do not be proud, but be diligent. The way of knowledge is ineffective. Learn to love. In loving God you transcend all things. Learn to preach

Christ. Do not even mention Kuling. After we disperse, each of our ways will be in the hand of God. He will keep us.

Finally, aside from the basic lessons for believers, the spirit of the gospel, the principles on authority, and other teachings, * let nothing else be mentioned. Share with those who are receptive. I sense that the road ahead of us is rather dark, but I believe there should be no problem for the consecrated. The Lord is the Lord above all. Let us learn to trust Him. Let us trust as well as love. God is full of mercy and glory. We delight to climb up to Him to serve Him. Do not be afraid nor be worried. Though we are but dust, yet we receive mercy to be allowed to participate in this glorious service. Let us thank God. In calling us to serve, God gives to us the greatest glory. There is no grace which is greater than this. Amen.

---

*Although these three and some other major series of spoken ministry had been delivered at the First Kuling Training Session a year earlier in 1948, the author in his Final Word above — and given a year later at the Second Training Session — is nevertheless found here gathering up into one as it were the teachings from both these Training Conferences.

The reader should be aware that the basic lessons for new believers are now available in English from Christian Fellowship Publishers in six volumes under the general title of the *Basic Lesson Series* (1972-75), the principles on authority are available under the title of *Spiritual Authority* (1972), while the spoken ministry referred to as the spirit of the gospel has just recently (1986) been translated and published under that very title. — *Translator*

PART THREE

A FEW LETTERS*

*Aside from one's speech nothing reveals a person more than a letter. The latter is informal, personal and intimate. In even only the few letters to follow, translated from the Chinese, we are given a valuable glimpse into the heart of the author. How faithful was this man to the motto he borrowed from sister Margaret E. Barber and chose for his own life: "I want nothing for myself; I want everything for the Lord." —*Translator*

1 | An Open Letter (January 1928)*

The imminent return of our Lord Jesus causes us to review many things in the light of the judgment seat. Is it too much to publish this magazine? If it is not of God we have no special reason to publish it, for it will only become a burden to the church and serve no purpose for God's true children. Yet we have received a commission from God to help His children — especially on spiritual life and spiritual warfare. So we have decided to publish this little paper. In each generation there is the needed truth for that time. We who live in this last age have doubtless our particular needed truth. This, then, is the aim of *The Present Testimony* magazine.

Within the limited pages of this periodical we intend to write on nothing but "the deep things of God" (1 Cor. 2.10). Various questions, ordinary teachings and

---

*This Open Letter appeared as the Editorial in the very first issue (January–February 1928) of *The Present Testimony* magazine that was published in Shanghai. — *Translator*

the meaning of Scripture texts — all these are good, but they are outside of the range we have set for ourselves. And hence, you must not expect to find such writings within the pages of this publication.

We strongly believe that now is the time of preparation. In order for God's children to be harvested they need first to ripen (see Mark 4.29). We would say that the time of rapture is near, but whether or not the church is ready looms as a major problem. The rapture of the Lord Jesus was an event which followed upon that of His cross. Can the church therefore travel along any other path? We sincerely believe that in this last hour God is leading His children to experience the cross of His Son more deeply so that they will be ready to ascend. God's present purpose is to speed up the completion of the testimony of His Son, the destruction of the Enemy, and the arrival of the kingdom. We trust that, in these few days left, God will gather His children in unity and that the church will not become a hindrance but, rather, a fellow-worker with Him towards the accomplishment of His eternal purpose. We humbly expect to be in God's hand and have a part in this glorious work.

The darkness in this current age is readily recognized by all who have eyes to see. What saddens our heart is the realization that were all which is "of man" to be taken away from the children of God there would be very little if anything left which would be "of God." What we see today is almost exclusively the works of man. Even in many beautiful works which people consider to be spiritual works, how much is really done by God himself? How pitiful that many works done "for the Lord," "in the name of God," "for the kingdom of God" or "for the church of Christ" are but the activities of man's corrupted flesh! These are done without seeking God's will, without receiving God's order, and without depending on God's power! The children of God simply do what *they* think is best! Everything is there except God. Thoughts, plans and efforts take the place of God. Unless God's children repent and return they shall one day discover how useless was their spiritual work, for they are destroying themselves as well as the work of God.

We know our wretchedness, but by the grace of God we want to be faithful. Our hope is that all who read these pages will do so without a spirit of criticism or a heart of secret gain but with a prayerful spirit and a humble heart. Only then will they be benefited somewhat by this paper. All that is written is written with but one aim, which is, that the readers — as those who live wholly in the new creation — may give themselves to God and become useful people in His hand. Accordingly, we singularly commit our writings, together with our readers as well as ourselves, to the God who can keep us eternally. May His Spirit lead us into all truths.

WATCHMAN NEE

2 | A Personal Letter (December 19, 1929)*

To all the brothers and sisters who have received the same calling in the Lord Jesus, greetings!

I have not met with you in this paper for over a year. I trust that you have learned from this publication as well as from other sources that I have been sick. Indeed, since 1926, my physical body has gotten weaker day by day. Due to many illnesses, plus many responsibilites, I could get no rest. Hence my health degenerated continuously. After I finished writing *The Spiritual Man* [June 1928], my strength was so exhausted that I have been bound by sickness ever since.

One thing I deeply regret is that during the last two years I have not been able to answer your letters on time, even having some letters remain unanswered. Although one or two brothers and sisters tried to briefly answer

---

*This appeared subsequently in *The Present Testimony* magazine.
  —*Translator*

my letters for me during my sickness, nevertheless many letters had to be left unattended to. For this I ask your forgiveness and understanding. You know that even at ordinary times I am kept busy enough; now, in sickness, I am naturally even more limited. I hope you will not mind my temporary untidiness.

Another thing for which I feel most grateful is that a few brothers and sisters in the Lord rendered to me, a lonely and helpless person, great service at the time of my distress. May the Lord richly reward them at the time of the resurrection of the righteous. There are also many brothers and sisters who know that I have no earthly possessions, and for the Lord's sake they have sent gifts to me — sacrificially and generously — from the North and the South [of China]. Thus I have had no lack during this sickness. Such generosity and affection is so great that I feel myself totally unworthy. I am but one of the most unprofitable servants of the Lord. Indeed, "ye sent once and again unto my need. . . . I seek for the fruit that increaseth to your account" (Phil. 4.16-17). What I hope is that your benevolence towards me may not be in vain. For I do wish that with this recovery I may fulfill my little part in God's business. Also, I want to express my gratitude to many brothers and sisters who are concerned and have written letters to me. May you all accept my grateful thanks.

No doubt what I have experienced in my affliction is most profitable to me. From the very beginning I have prayed that God would cause me to learn what I should learn in this sickness. I do not wish to be ill in vain. As I look back over the past year or so, I can say with deep gratitude that God has been right in treating me thus. Not even one day could have been omitted. Naturally, many of my experiences are too personal to be shared openly, yet I deeply trust that all are for the benefit of others as well as for myself.*

Now, through the endless and boundless grace of God and through your unceasing prayers, I have once again come back from the gate of death. I expect God to fully recover me in His due time. So, I am now resting in work. I once again offer myself to God to do His will and to serve His saints. Many things concerning my own future may have to change. There may be changes in the literary work, in local work, and in outside work. I and my fellow-workers are at present waiting upon the Lord. We are willing to give deeper obedience to more light. We will inform you as soon as "the pattern in the mount" is made clear to us. Ever

---

*Doubtless this paragraph is a direct allusion to what, among other matters, the author had only just recently explained in his two Prefaces (dated June 4, 1927 and June 25, 1928) which he had penned for the three-volume work already mentioned above entitled *The Spiritual Man*, and which was published in Chinese just prior to his composing the above letter. In these Prefaces the author described for his readers something of the nature and dimensions of the sickness, the afflictions, and the battling against the Enemy which he had been experiencing throughout the long period just before and during the drafting of this monumental work on spiritual life and warfare of the Christian. The author's great desire and prayer, enunciated repeatedly in the Prefaces, was, that such experiences would not simply be for his own benefit but perhaps even more importantly would be for the blessing of his readers. He recognized the absolute necessity that he go through such a

since the conference that was held in February of last year, many people have been asking us when we would be having the next conference, for they wish to come. At present we are not able to say anything. This must wait until we know the Lord's mind.

Beloved brethren, the second coming of the Lord is imminent. We must be faithful. In spite of the possibility of more misunderstanding and fiercer opposition, which are foreordained, we need to be faithful. Apostasy will increase, and many will fall away; darkness will deepen, and we will be more ill-treated; but all these things tell us that the Lord is near. In these days the word of God is: "He that is unrighteous, let him do unrighteousness still: and he that is filthy, let him be made filthy still: and he that is righteous, let him do righteousness still: and he that is holy, let him be made holy still" (Rev. 22.11). Brethren, please con-

---

crucible of trials so that what his book's readers might read would not be based on *theory* but on *experience* which had been wrought out in the life of the writer. He had at one point even discontinued writing the book for three years chiefly because he wished to afford an opportunity for this to become a reality in certain areas of his life where it was lacking before he would once again resume the composition of the book.

The readers of this present volume may wish to consult the English translation of this significant work under discussion: Watchman Nee, *The Spiritual Man*, 3 vols. (New York: Christian Fellowship Publishers, originally translated from the Chinese and published in 1968; but a Combined (3 vols-in-1) Edition, 1977 is now the only format of the book available from the Publishers). —*Translator*

tinue to remember me and pray for me that I may stand faithfully in such trial and bear a good witness for God.

> *Just a few more miles, beloved,*
>   *And our feet shall ache no more;*
> *No more sin, and no more sorrow,*
>   *Hush, thee, Jesus went before;*
> *And I hear Him sweetly whispering,*
>   *"Fear not, fear not, still press on,*
> *For it may be ere tomorrow,*
>   *The long journey will be done."*

—M. E. BARBER

Peace be to you.

Bondservant of Christ,

WATCHMAN NEE

3 | An Open Letter (March 12, 1930)*

Brothers and sisters in the household of faith:

It is good to receive grace from God, but it is equally important not to forget the grace of God. For this reason, we must be attentive to our responsibility and careful about our work so as to glorify God's name. Currently, *The Present Testimony* has entered into its third consecutive year of being published in Shanghai. We wish to take this opportunity to talk about this publication.

We may say that there are many magazines being published today. Each has its responsibility and aim. Many spiritual teachings and Biblical commentaries to be found in them are most helpful. Yet these are not our ministry. Others may be called to do these, but they

---

*This appeared subsequently as the Editorial in the issue of *The Present Testimony* magazine that was to follow.—*Translator*

are not within the measure which the Lord has given to us. We are not willing to cross the boundary and step into others' territories.

What we see is that in the church of God today there is a principal lack, which is, knowing Christ and Him crucified. For this theme is not just an event in history; it is God's unchangeable spiritual principle to be proven experientally by His church. We consider this to be the center of all truths. All the other questions and matters are but accessories. For this reason we proclaim only God's spiritual principles in our publication without touching Biblical interpretation and other subjects. These latter are good, but they are not our work. The Lord has taught us not to argue and strive. In striving we will fall from spiritual position. The lack today is life. This is true individually; this is also true corporately. We lack the resurrection life of Christ — that life which overcomes death, the grave and Hades.

How sad that almost all Bible terms have lost their original meanings. The words remain the same, but the things they signify are vastly different. The power spoken of today is not the power spoken of previously. The work today is no longer the work of yesterday. Formerly, people were baptized into the death of Christ; now, baptism has become a sacrament. Formerly, laying on of hands was for identification; now it has become a ritual. Formerly, what was filled with life and spiritual reality has now become a kind of empty ceremony. Though the church may still be active in preaching the gospel and in missionary work, its power today lags far behind what it was previously. Therefore, today's need is to be filled with the life of the Lord and to enter into spiritual reality. When life comes, all the lifeless terms used nowadays shall become experiences.

As a consequence, our aim in this new publication is centered upon this. Although many secondary issues are indeed urgent, we will not divide our attention. For we confess that if God's children are filled with the resurrection life of Christ, all these secondary issues shall automatically be solved. However, the ground for resurrection is death. The theme of death and resurrection is God's principle. This is why we stress much on preaching the fact and principle of co-death with Christ. We know some may accept the principle (in experience) and forget the fact, and others may believe in the fact yet neglect the principle. Both will result in a lopsided life. The attempt to follow the principle of co-death without believing the fact of co-death is a kind of spiritual suicide. Yet merely believing in the fact of the believer's co-death without following in life the principle of co-death — such faith is but spiritual idealism. We therefore emphasize both sides.

We know we are now bearing a solitary testimony. In the present day of love waning, teachers multiplying, and ears itching, we realize that our testimony will be rejected by many people. Nonetheless, we consider such isolation to be worthwhile. We are able to stand alone because we stand on God's side. We thank God for giving us not a few friends in the past days and years. We thank you for your sympathy. Furthermore, there are many who have written to us and told us how they are praying for us.

During the past two years we have sent out nearly thirty thousand copies of *The Present Testimony* magazine. Although we have never directly or indirectly asked for help in meeting the financial needs of printing and distributing it, God has moved the hearts of His children to send in funds and help the publishing. We thank God especially for the fact that we have not received big donations or donations from wealthy people; what we have received are gifts of a few dollars, a few dimes and a few cents contributed by ordinary believers. Since God has supplied us in such a way in the days gone by, we believe He will be just as faithful in the days ahead.

In the past two years we have also sent out tens of thousands of gospel tracts. Sometimes we have heard of people getting saved through these tracts. Though the cost was high, thank God, He has not allowed us to be in lack. Not even once were we unable to pay our bill. We always paid off immediately. We will continue with this work, and we expect to send out even more tracts than in the years before. We want to use this opportunity to thank our brothers and sisters who have helped us in this work.

As regards the books I have personally written and which the Gospel Book Room has published, let me say a few words to clear up some rumors. Ever since the Lord had called me to serve Him I have seen one thing, which is, that I should not receive any wages in preaching the gospel for the Lord. The leprosy that cleaved to Gehazi (see 2 Kings 5.20–27) is my constant warning. So that in these years, apart from some voluntary gifts sent by people to me as they were moved by the Spirit of the Lord, I have never received a penny for my oral or written messages. Though I have written some books, still these have not increased my income; rather, they have required my subsidy. I really should not say these words, yet even as Paul was, I (though most unworthy) am forced to say them. The apostle considered his words "I preached to you the gospel of God for nought" as "that which I speak, I speak not after the Lord, but as in foolishness, in this confidence of glorying" (2 Cor. 11.7b,17); yet once again he declared, "I am become foolish: ye compelled me" (2 Cor. 12.11).

Concerning some sisters and one brother who are my fellow-workers, allow me to speak frankly. None of them depends on the Gospel Book Room for their livelihood. They all look to God to supply their needs. Even though their needs are not known to men, yet up to today God has not allowed them to go into debt. These few fellow-workers, as did the apostles before them, have their times "both to abound and to be in want" (Phil. 4.12); nonetheless, when we look back over these years, we cannot but say, "Ebenezer" (1 Sam. 7.12).

With regard to myself, I am still resting on the one hand and working on the other. In spite of the many things I am yet unable to do, I thank God for what I can do. In the matter of a special conference, we do not have any plans at present. In case there were one, accommodations would be a problem because so many want to come. Concerning the numerous Bible questions many people have written to me about, I have to speak frankly that I am unable to answer them. If I were to answer all of them, I suppose I would have to open a Bible correspondence course. However, I will seek time to answer problems on spiritual life.

Some asked about the new translation of the New Testament published in Nanking. According to my view, it is not as good as the Chinese Union version published by the Bible Society. In this hour of many confused voices, we need to be careful about privately published Bibles.

We felt great sorrow as we received news of the home-going of Miss M. E. Barber of Lo-hsing Pagoda, Pagoda Anchorage.* She was one of the deepest in the Lord. To me, her communion with the Lord and her loyalty to the Lord were rare in this world. By reading the poem on the cover page of this issue [see immediately below], you can know this saint.

A bondservant of Christ,

WATCHMAN NEE

If the path I travel
    Lead me to the cross,
If the way Thou choosest
    Lead to pain and loss,
Let the compensation
    Daily, hourly, be
Shadowless communion,
    Blessed Lord, with Thee.

---

*Lo-hsing Pagoda was located at the tip of an island situated in the River Min opposite to Pagoda Anchorage, downriver and closer to the South China Sea from the large port city of Foochow, the birthplace of Watchman Nee.—*Translator*

If there's less of earth joy,
  Give, Lord, more of heaven.
Let the spirit praise Thee,
  Though the heart be riven;
If sweet earthly ties, Lord,
  Break at Thy decree,
Let the tie that binds us,
  Closer, sweeter, be.

Lonely though the pathway,
  Cheer it with Thy smile;
Be Thou my companion
  Through earth's little while;
Selfless may I live, Lord,
  By Thy grace to be
Just a cleansèd channel
  For Thy life through me.

—M. E. BARBER

4 | A Personal Letter (June 17, 1930)*

Beloved brothers and sisters:

I rejoice in my heart for our ability to send out another issue of *The Present Testimony*. I firmly believe that the testimony of the death and resurrection of the Lord Jesus is the urgent need of today. Our hope is that God's children will appropriate what the death and resurrection of Christ have accomplished for us, in order that we may so completely overcome sin, the world and Satan that we may testify that our Lord is alive, that He is indeed risen. There is no testimony in a defeated life, no matter how much truth that one has absorbed in his mind. For this very reason, nay, for the glory of God, we send out this issue.

Nevertheless, our attitude is not that of standing on a lofty platform and preaching to other people. No, no, for we also preach to ourselves, even preaching to

---

*This appeared in the July 1930 issue of *The Present Testimony* magazine. —*Translator*

ourselves first. It is for the sake of mutual admonition that we write these pages. We dare not say that we have it all or that we are perfect; rather, we wish to pursue and press on towards the goal with God's countless children. Irrespective of our personal achievement, we believe what things are written within these pages are truths. We further believe that these are truths precious to us. I hope my readers will prayerfully read this issue so that they may obtain all which is stated herein.

I would also like to take this opportunity to say something about myself. As I write this letter I am on Kuling mountain in Kiangsi Province.* Through the loving kindness of a foreign missionary, I find myself in a quiet and cool house. Two years ago she lent me this house, and this year she once again let me use it. For this I am most grateful. Due to my nerve and physical conditions, I am not able to stay on the plain in the summer time. And to spend some time each year to be quiet before God, to learn prayer as well as to receive revelation, is also indispensable. I thank God's children and my fellow-workers for their special care of me so that I have no problem staying here. I know that during the summer many readers, too, will come to the mountain. I hope they will visit me only from ten to twelve in the mornings, inasmuch as I have other

---

*This is not to be confused with Mount Kuling in Fukien Province near the city of Foochow which became famous, during the latter years of the author's ministry, as the site for the Training Conferences he convened there in 1948 and 1949 for fellow-workers. This other Kuling mountain is far to the northwest of Foochow some 600 miles up the Yangtze River and just south of the river port of Kiukiang.—*Translator*

things to do during the rest of the day.* My address here is Number 103.**

As regards my other personal problems, I may perhaps make some changes according to my friends' advice and my own physical health. After much prayer and consideration, I now seem to have some idea. But I do not know how God will arrange everything.

At present I have a very deep conviction, and that is, that God's children lack a living experience of Christ. As a consequence, they are not willing to spend energy and money on sinners. The coming of the Lord Jesus is imminent, and the testimony of God's Son must be spread without delay. Beloved, just realize how we are but lowly insects, and yet the God of creation calls us to be partakers of His Son's rejection. How wonderful this is! How rare and how very short is this opportunity! Today may be the last day; who can tell? Who can say that the Lord will not come today to receive His children

---

*Actually, unknown to his vistors, the rest of the day he was fairly much occupied with simply lying "flat on his back" due to his severe physical debilitation. See Angus I. Kinnear, *Against the Tide: the Story of Watchman Nee* (Eastbourne, England: Victory Press, 1973), p. 82.—*Translator*

**House No. 103, which belonged to a lady foreign missionary based in Nanking, was situated a little ways down the mountainside where was located the Chinese market-town known as "the Gap" (itself at 3,500′ a.s.l.). It will be of interest to readers of Watchman Nee that it was at a nearby house to No. 103 where lived the humble mechanic and his wife who were brought to the Lord by the author during this time and who figured centrally in the now celebrated and touching *Resident Boss* story so greatly appreciated by many Christians the world over, and recounted in several of the Nee books (e.g., in *The Normal Christian Life*). —*Translator*

home? For this reason, we must, as never before, seek after the lost sheep for the Lord's sake. God has only one Son, who is a Preacher. Ought we not preach also?

For you who have earthly wealth, I exhort you to offer generously to the Lord. What grieves me is that many wealthy people give a few dollars and a few dimes instead of hundreds and thousands of dollars, while poor people offer much more. While their gold and silver rust away, the work of God suffers. God's workmen are in want, with the bottom of their purses bare; nonetheless, they accumulate their wealth for eternity where there shall be no want. We ought to know that both the way we *use* money and the way we do *not* use money will be judged.

Of course, I am not persuading you to contribute to unfruitful endeavors, for many workers are no longer God's workmen and many works are no longer God's work. What I am saying is that we must take care of those who truly go out in the name of the Lord, who are trusting the Lord for their living without accepting anything from the heathen. So far as I know, there are at least several dozen people in that category, and tremendous are their needs! Nevertheless, rich believers are negligent in supporting them.

The next issue of our publication will closely follow this one. May the Lord bless this paper. Brethren, I need your prayers very much. Please pray with faith for me.

Peace be unto you.

A bondservant of Christ,

WATCHMAN NEE

5 | A Personal Letter (February 28, 1931)*

I have not contacted you for several months. I thank God for giving me rest in Him and for enabling me to take up work responsibility again. God really used my sickness in the last two to three years to test the heart of many saints. My weakness has become the occasion of the love of many towards the Lord. As I think of your lovingkindness, how grateful I am! I heard that many brothers and sisters, scattered in various places, who have not known me in the flesh and yet because of the relationship created in Christ, cry with tears before God on behalf of my health. This causes me to sense how much you have given me and how little I have served you. It also induces me to say that had I more life, strength and time, I would most willingly spend all for the saints.

---

*This was entitled, "A Letter to My Beloved Readers," and appeared in the January–February 1931 issue of *The Present Testimony* magazine.—*Translator*

My body's hurt is the accumulation of many years. It was further aggravated by writing *The Spiritual Man.** But, thank God, I am now slowly recovering. I am able again to write a few letters, prepare a few articles, lead a few Bible studies, and attend a few meetings. Although I expect to do more, yet in spite of the many things I cannot do, I ought to thank God for what I can do. According to various experts on health, I have been adjudged dead several times. Thank God, I am still alive today. I hope in my days of sojourning I may serve Him and you faithfully.

In connection with my fellow-workers in Shanghai, I would like to say a few words concerning the aim of our work. We sense deeply that the need of the churches in China today is to know what is true spiritual work and what is the way that God's children must walk before Him. Our desire is to contact those everywhere who are hungry for the Lord and to help them. As regards *The Present Testimony* magazine, some may perhaps consider it to be too deep and too focused. Yet this paper is designed to supply what other publications which are greatly used of the Lord do not supply. This is confirmed by the letters written to us by many readers. Consequently, we are assured that we are not mistaken in the commission which we received from the Lord. By the grace of the Lord, this year and in the years to come (if He wills), this publication will continue to deal with the deep things of God.

The gospel tracts which we publish have been truly

---

*See the lengthy footnote appended to the 19 December 1929 letter above for an explanation of this further aggravation. —*Translator*

blessed of the Lord. In the last two to three years we have sent out more than five million of them, and this year we have already printed one and a half million. Even so, there has been no shortage in meeting the cost of printing. Though we have never asked for donations nor received any foundation, God has put in the heart of men the need of this work. Here and there some money was sent to us, enabling us to fulfill what God had ordered us to do. We do thank Him with all our hearts.

Regarding the article on "Self-Knowledge and the Light of God"* in this issue, this is an indispensable knowledge for God's children today who would walk in His way. May God use this to liberate the bound. May you readers pray much in reading this article.

Friends, there is not much time left! Our Lord is at the doors! [see Matt. 24.33] May we use this last opportunity to commit ourselves to the will of God and allow Him to lead us to the place of His choice. May we be faithful lest we regret when we look back from eternity. He loved us and gave himself up for us. He is therefore worthy to have our all. May our eyes be fixed on the Lord who is not here.

Peace be to you.

A bondservant of Christ,

WATCHMAN NEE

---

*This article was translated into English and published under the same title, appearing as Part Two of Watchman Nee, *Spiritual Knowledge* (New York: Christian Fellowship Publishers, 1973), pp. 45–82. —*Translator*

6 | An Open Letter (March 23, 1933)*

Now is truly an hour of temptation. Everything is confused, cold and cruel. It is really hard for Christians to stand at this time. But, did we not know this beforehand? What, then, can we say?

Though we may be dragging ourselves along the way or looking about with bewilderment, how can we lay down our weapons if we have not been raptured? O Lord, what do You think best?

This is the first issue of the new year of publication. We cannot say we have greater expectation, greater courage or greater interest than that which accompanied the publication of those issues that appeared last year. Quite the contrary, we are fearful for greater difficulty. In spite of all, we must press on.

We treasure prayer partners.

WATCHMAN NEE

---

*This appeared in the somewhat delayed January–February 1933 issue of *The Present Testimony* magazine.—*Translator*

7 | The Last Letter — Written from Prison Camp*

Elder sister Ping-tseng:

Your letter dated April 7 [1972] was received. I understand that you have not received my letter in which I told you that I did receive the things you sent me each time. I did get the things you mentioned in your letter. I am really grateful to you.

You know my physical condition. Mine is a chronic disease; it is organic. When it is active, it is most painful; but even when it is dormant, it is still there. The difference lies in its being active or dormant, not in having or not having. The summer now arrives. By being exposed more to the sunlight, my skin may change some

---

*In April 1952 the author, aged 48, was arrested in Manchuria by the Chinese Communist government. He was subsequently "tried" *in absentia* on false charges at a series of so-called "accusation" or condemnation meetings which were held between January and June 1956 in Shanghai. Only at the final proceeding, on 21 June, did he himself — still a prisoner of the State — appear before the High Court, which again was not to be a public trial but simply

color, but my sickness remains the same. However, I maintain my joy. Hence, please do not worry about me. I hope you would take better care of yourself and may your heart be filled with joy.

SHU-TSU
(Watchman Nee's childhood name)

---

a public meeting, at which he was finally found guilty, condemned and sentenced to 15 years' imprisonment with reform by labor, such sentence to run from 12 April 1952. This was afterwards extended for five more years. His wife, Charity Nee, who was the only person permitted to visit him, died in early October 1971. In the meanwhile the author had been moved (in January 1970) from the Shanghai Central Jail to a labor camp in Anhwei Province far to the west of Shanghai. It was from here that he penned the above letter, dated 22 April 1972, addressed to his sister-in-law. It proved to be his last. He was 68 when he died on June 1, 1972.—*Translator*